Pivotal Moments

By Dr. Ray A. Seamons

Pivotal Moments

A collection of personal reflections at various defining moments.

ISBN: 978-1-936799-03-9

Cover photo **Luke Hansen Photography**

Contents

FOREWORD

Life doesn't always turn out the way we had planned. In fact, the best laid plans are sure to be thwarted by misfortune, sickness, miscommunication, environmental issues, and a multitude of other unforeseen obstacles. As we age, we come to see such challenges as part of the mortal experience. If we are open to it, lessons can be learned through these roadblocks, and we can become more compassionate and understanding towards others. As I am now well into mid-life, I find that much of what I once thought was important to own, to achieve, and to experience, no longer holds me hostage. I have let go of many of the beliefs held by the post-war generation of high-achieving, better-than-our-parents, pie-in-the-sky people. The reflections collected here are merely the result of personal evaluations of self and societal values when dealing with the various vicissitudes life has thrown my way. It is my hope that my personal struggles and resultant thoughts may serve as a catalyst to help another on the path through life.

1. MY CHILD

You are my child. You are unique. You are special. You are one of a kind, an individual. Your birth was a celebration. Each accomplishment of your development added to the joy which makes up the rich memory of my life. You are my meaning, but not an object or possession. You are not a means to fulfill my emptiness, but rather the whole purpose for my being. You are the select blend of your mother and my genetic codes; a little bit of this and a portion of that. You have been placed to grow alongside your brothers and sisters who are similar, yet individual. You share characteristics and aspects of personality from a long line of great people who are linked to a royal lineage of grand lives and prestigious souls. Not everything you will experience will be positive. Not everything you will experience will be pleasant. Yet, all of it is necessary to make you who you will become. Loved equally as a member of the family, yet valued and cherished as individuals, you must go and find your destiny, be it great or small. Spread your wings, stretch them long and wide. Soar with the best, and don't fear failure. This life is but a short time. The saddest thing is not to fail but the remorse of saying, "It might have been." My love for you is real. Love is not a quantity to be measured and dispensed; it is an unending, expanding gift. Without end, it cannot be taken. Once given it is there for eternity embedded deep within the very fibers of our souls. I will hold this gift of knowing you close to my heart for eternity. You are not alone. You matter. You are my child.

* * * * *

2. IT'S NOT FAIR

Some are born to privilege, but most will live without.
Many are born healthy, while frailties leave others in doubt.
Few will rule the kingdom, as most must fall to their reign.
Some will live for moments, and few will feel no pain.
When this earth life is over, will we all be judged the same?

Few attain great callings, while select may change the world.
Most will worship possessions, with prideful banners unfurled.
We're told where much is given, much will be required.
Am I a grateful servant, or does envy make me tired?
Do I perform my duty, to be seen before my peers?
Is my heart pure and true, or am I ruled by my fears?
When my days are over, will my works be judged by men?
With an eraser I can change things, unless it was written in pen.

* * * * *

3. THE POLE BENDS

My Dad was a great outdoorsman. If it flew, crawled, ran, walked, or swam it should be tracked, caught, and cooked. Fishing was one of his favorite activities. The rod, the reel, the line, and the tackle were all important, all unique, all chosen for an event's specific outcomes. Unfortunately, I extracted more in metaphor than in skill from the outdoor lessons he sought to teach me. I thus conclude that life is and always has been a struggle, apparently by design. The struggle is not just for me, but for all who have occupied or will occupy this globe. The fishing pole bends heavier for some than others, and no one has yet figured out why. The greater the fight, the greater the excitement, but in turn the greater the struggle and often the disappointment. Just as you never know when you make a cast if what attacks your fly is a minnow or a marlin, we wrestle with the rod of life just the same. Like the fish on your line, when it's there you feel it, you fight it, you gain line, you lose line, you carry on until the line breaks, the pole snaps, the fish escapes, or it's landed. Regardless of the outcome, when the tension is gone the struggle is over, but the experience will be relived time and time again. Having left a permanent imprint on your very soul, it will be continually referenced throughout your existence because of the intensity of the struggle that occurred. My Dad lived such a life up to the very end. It wasn't easy but it was full of excitement, full of energy, and full of growth. As a fifteen year old I watched as his last breath was released. At that tender age, I scarcely comprehended the impact of his life upon me, but it was understood that his legacy would not be forgotten.

* * * * *

4. TOLERANCE

Throughout my life I've felt isolated from discrimination. A sensation of belonging, an awareness of presence, and a feeling of inclusion has always attended me. I naturally assumed this sense of equality was experienced by all. Friends, many from various nationalities, were effortlessly considered as valued peers. In quiet moments, many times they would share thoughts of non-inclusion and inequality. Listening patiently, I emotionally discredited their feelings as being overly sensitive. I concluded that it was insensitivity, not malicious intent, that was the source of the insult.

I've always considered myself tolerant and accepting. Prejudice was never something I could comprehend. Diversity provides richness and depth to any engagement, and something to be valued. Having never been the minority, I was protected from inadequacy, insufficiency, and failure. Feeling accepted, it was easy to be accepting. I have recently begun to sense the discomfort of bigotry first-hand. Surprisingly this feedback comes from those who profess to know better. Life changes have resulted in an alteration in my social status. I now find myself feeling isolated, disenfranchised, and different. Now the exception instead of the rule, even the simplest transactions seem to exclude me. Real or perceived, most likely both, the hurt leads to paranoia and increased sensitivity that in turn promotes additional pain. This vicious cycle can become all consuming if not kept in check.

Our journey through life is not without incident. Intent is often overridden by chance occurrences or blindness. Can people worldwide overcome their biases and rectify their thoughtlessness? My soul screams, "Yes," but my experience shouts, "NO!" Societal expectations appear unforgiving. Like the color of my skin or the accent in my voice, am I now marked for life? Am I now different, strange, and foreign? I find myself critical of the judgments in an attempt to redeem self and justify the past. Shunned and forsaken, the warmth which in times past drew me near, has now turned cold and isolating. It's natural to reject after having been once rejected. This trend has only one end, which outcome I refuse to accept. So what do I do? How do I co-exist with the superficial? Can I stop this out-bound inclination? Can I arrest this process, which so rapidly erodes my confidence? Which will win, self-preservation, or understanding and maturity? I pray for support, for strength, and for courage to choose tolerance and understanding.

* * * * *

5. TOO OLD SMART

I have a few miles on the odometer now. Not yet ready for a trade-in, but I'm well past time for a major tune up. I need to evaluate all the systems: cooling, electrical, mechanical. It's the internal issues that worry me. Hidden deep within the drive train, who can know what the true condition is? There are indicators which can be used to determine relative health. The amount and color of the fluids, considered with the general overall use, is about the best determinant.

I was hard on my body in youth. The careless habits when young have given way to the pains of middle age. I am now a little slower to get up from kneeling. The silhouette of younger days has fallen prey to gravity. I can't see my feet without leaning way out. But, what about the hidden aspects of my soul? Arrogant, abrasive behaviors have mellowed over time. My urgency to impress has relented to a desire to observe and reflect. Once so sure of my facts, now everything appears to be less clear cut and relative. The obvious has succumbed to the obscure.

While deep in thought during one of these annual tune-ups, I notice that what I once thought was within specification is now possibly being interpreted wrongly. Coldness grips my heart and my face flushes. Could I have been misreading something as important as this for so long? The new found truth causes two simultaneous reactions. I must change my behavior for the future, but what about my past? What damage have I unintentionally caused? I meant well, but that just wasn't enough. What internal damage and hurt has been caused due to my personal blindness? Now I see more clearly and will approach things with greater sensitivity, but what about the damage to date? Oh, if I could but re-live a few select moments of my life's history. This remorse can be beneficial by encouraging me to work that much harder in the present. The energy and excitement to get there fast is now replaced with the stability and peace of getting there safely. At least I caught it before more harm was done. But now I wonder if there are other things established firmly in my personality that are out of adjustment, unseen, or misread? Better catch them today before more injury is caused.

* * * * *

6. WAVES OF REALITY

Living lives of delusion, we proceed ahead confidant that our personal perspective is reality and not an artifact of biased, synthesized thought mingled with selective truth. Formulated through a mix of undisputed fact, personal perspective, and emotional need, "vital lies" are generated promising reasonable, probable, and likely closure. We aggressively proceed ahead as if our recent conception of fabricated reality is real, tangible, and sure. Surrounded by people of similar thought, or by those who are easily manipulated, our falsehoods are reinforced. The well-rehearsed "half truths," for the purpose of self-preservation, automatically adjust the story 24/7 to the onslaught of diverging facts, all in preservation of ego. It would seem that the greater the insecurity the greater the effort toward self-maintenance.

Regardless of our skill and determination toward ego-preservation, we all confront waves of reality in life. These are the massive indisputable events which force truth down upon our illusions and self-esteem, knocking down the pilings of our unsubstantiated perspectives. Waves of reality are a natural phenomenon of life. Their devastation is in direct proportion to the degree of reality we are operating under. To those "far-a-field" and void of truth, the waves are overwhelming. To the unaware, the clueless, and the innocent, they are caught asleep. Once awakened, they can choose to accept, incorporate, and change, or to deny, reject, and dig-in with intense rationalization. A few, the prepared and the healthy, are open to the possibility of personal failings, limitations, biases, and delusions. As such, the waves do not destroy them. The potentially destructive energy can be used for refinement, improvement, and modification. The goal is not to preserve personal delusions, but to discover reality. Their foundation is grounded not on sand but in the bedrock of certainty. Over years of introspection, they are eager to accept truth, and easily reject spite. Each incoming wave pounds the pilings deeper, stronger, and purer.

As the swells of life begin to form in the distance, are we aware of their implications? As they deepen and spell danger, are we threatened? As the waves progress toward our shoreline, does fear emerge? As the energy is released upon our dock, do we resist and reject, or accept and improve? I, alone, am the one who can tell.

True growth comes in minute adjustments and incremental improvements. Awareness of the present appears to be the strong beginning. Cut free of personal illusions and facades we sit naked, exposed, and vulnerable. This is the beginning of personal awareness that leads to acceptance of self and circumstances. This is more than a begrudging tolerance of my life, but a pleasant healthy approval of who I am, why I'm here, where I came from, what I can do to improve, and how I will proceed. This process is paramount to the results. Given time, I will grow strong; not like the cottonwood tree whose rapid uncontrolled growth makes it vulnerable to wind and storm, but more like the slow growing oak which is ridged, strong and ready for the long haul.

* * * * *

7. CHANGE

If a system, organization, or behavior remains untouched, does it not stand to reason that the outcomes will also remain constant? We continue to perform our routines without change, but we hope that the outcomes will be different, better, and purer.

It requires two Chinese characters to convey the notion of change: one is danger, and the other is opportunity. Our personal attitude toward change is a huge factor in how we manage it. On a good day, even the advocates of a change are rarely more than mildly excited when considering the work required. Then there are the opponents who perceive the new process or behavior to be negative to their current safety and security. Altering the course of a great ocean liner, once set in motion, is slow and deliberate. The momentum must be diverted and modified. Time then validates this course. So it is with many of us: change is slow and deliberate. Change can also be sporadic. This irregular change arrives often without notice, throwing existing processes and comfort out of whack. By controlling desires and planning for change, we are consciously able to alter behavior.

Einstein concluded that it was the definition of insanity to expect different results from the same behavior. How often do we fall into this very trap? It is easy to follow habitual patterns of life where we desire change, yet are overwhelmed by the fear of change removing us from the safe, the predictable, and the known. Emotions run on overload as we crave the potential of change, the desire for change, and the need for change, yet safety, fear of the unknown, and doubt stand in our way. A personal hell is created through discontent as we deny our potential. Self-loathing is generated through weakness, and our unmet expectations linger forever. Oh, if only we could feel peace and contentment with mediocrity!

Trapped in our current course many of us lack the reserves to reassess, recalibrate, and revise our own behavior. Until there is a complete and successful transition with the old behavior being laid aside and the new in place, pressure will continue to increase. Never without challenge, successful change requires closure. Initial planning requires assessing total costs, budgeting time, and consistently measuring and validating progress. This requires a crystal clear picture of who we currently are in light of a vision of who we want to be. The difference between the two becomes the project description that is operationally defined, meaningful, measurable, and time bound.

* * * * *

8. 90 MILES FROM CUBA

While on business in Florida I was enjoying the scenery, the climate, and the weather. Even in the middle of December it is fantastic there: deep greens, rich blues, blinding whites, and miles and miles of golden sand separating the ocean from the sky. Pink, orange, and coral red sunsets complement the entire picture.

A rental car, a full tank of gas, and some time led us south. Passing theme parks to national forests, curiosity carried us closer and closer to the equator. South of Miami is a string of islands called the Keys; they reach 120 miles into the Caribbean. Beginning with Key Largo, we soon found ourselves driving further and further south. "Just one more," I'd tell myself, "then I'll turn back." But in spite of my personal counsel I proceeded on; one Key, then another, and another. The sun began to set over the Gulf and before I realized it we were well committed to see this thing to the end. Later on that evening I arrived at the end of the road. Originally built as a Navel Air Station during World War II, Key West has become a poplar tourist stop for cruise ships negotiating the Caribbean. Upon arriving, I secured lodging and went to work exploring the night life. Two ships were in port and the old town was alive with action.

The next morning we continued our exploration. Following the beaches south we eventually stumbled upon a land marker. Erected to designate the Southern-most tip of the United States, it read: "90 miles to CUBA." Wait! I didn't want to go to CUBA! CUBA is probably the last place in the world I wanted to be near. I was now closer to Guantanamo Bay and Fidel Castro than Miami and Uncle Sam. A strange feeling came over me. How did this happen? How did I end up here, 90 miles from CUBA? Why on earth would anyone want to be 90 miles from CUBA! Even the Cubans were swimming in the opposite direction.

I gazed out across the bright blue expanse and pondered. Sitting down on the warm white sand I began to consider my actions. How did I get so far from my intended destination? How did I get so off track from my overall objective? At what moment was the decision made which brought me here? I didn't recall making a definitive choice in the matter. I never planned out this journey in detail. So how did it happen? I'm a reasonable guy, and although extemporaneous at times I had never been hit with a situation as insightful as this. After some time in reflecting on the matter it hit me: I got here ONE MILE AT A TIME! Curiosity, justification, and non-commitment all combined to delay my course change, and each ensuing mile made the detour more determined. "One Mile at a Time" added up to bring me here. "One Mile at a Time," while insignificant in and of themselves, possessed the additive effect of a major course deviation. This is so much like life: distractions, curiosity, and pleasure combine to slowly, subtly, and surely alter our plans. We become so easily distracted, so quickly led off course, and so slow to respond. But, how dramatic are the results: 90 miles from CUBA.

I'll remember this for some time to come. Times when I catch my mind beginning to wander and when curiosity begins to offset reason. So what now? Shall I rent a boat and finish the last leg of the unintended journey, or shall I regroup and return? Regardless of my choice I will not arrive immediately. The voyage from this point on will proceed as in the past "One Mile at a Time." Regrets of time lost, longing for past situations, impatient for restoration, and frustrated for lost opportunities, none of these will expedite the journey. I resolve to the fact that "it is what it is," and as such, I might as well enjoy the ride.

* * * * *

9. WATERED DOWN ORANGE JUICE

My mother was a master at the art of extending stuff and making do. My father died in my youth, and as such things were always tight financially. Mom did not want us to do without, yet she lacked the resources to do it right. Thus, everything was extended: our raw milk was mixed with powdered, the meat loaf was 90% bread, and the orange juice was light yellow water. The scant pieces of pulp ensured us all that it contained some real juice; it was just the concentration that was in question.

I'm not against watering things down or diluting issues when appropriate. Even today I don't enjoy concentrated events. Mom's orange juice did originate as frozen concentrate; she just went a bit too far in my mind. Even though her heart was in the right place, her extreme watering-down of the subject often resulted in missing the point. The politically correct are masters of this dilution process where critical issues are addressed, but the pulp is gone and the color is pale at best. There is an exact moment at which mom's OJ ceased to become juice. At this point it turned into colored water.

Issues in our personal communications confront this same challenge. Have you ever sat down and eaten the frozen concentrate straight out of the can with a spoon? You can't take many bites until the lips pucker and you experience brain freeze. Blunt, undiluted truth is hard to digest. When everything observed is openly spoken, response is low and listeners naturally reject or factor down the information. On the other hand, excessive diluting completely changes the intent. Watering down the content results in missed issues and bypassed objectives.

The dilution ratio of all orange juice concentrate, as stated on the can, is intended to maximize consumption. The objective of the consumer is to maximize value. Knowing the nutritional value of fruit juice in the growth of children, Mom's original purpose was to supply us with such nourishment. Yet, given her limited budget, her conflicting objective was to minimize consumption. Thus the dilution process began. I don't know when the liquid she created ceased to have dietary value. Somewhere along the way, taste and color lost presence, and uncertainty prevailed. Heck, if it had tasted better and looked more inviting we would have wanted more. As I reflect upon mom's juice I conclude that she meant us no physical harm. As a mother, her need to provide was strong, and she did the best that she could. Our mutual purpose may not have been met but the love was there. I see that now.

* * * * *

10. SACRED SPACES

The world is full of sacred spaces that commemorate human greatness, sacrifice, and honor. These places represent moments in the flood of humankind's existence when we have stood taller, walked straighter, and embraced deeper. These places provide opportunities to lovingly reflect upon the events that transpired at such spaces, which in turn inspires us to over-achieve and out-perform. Often these spaces represent scenes of bloodshed, sacrifice, and pain. Emotions run unchecked as we reflect upon such events. As the tear stained ground speaks to us today we are invited to remember. Remember, oh, please, remember. An unspoken reverence attends these spaces in honor of those great souls who sacrificed all so that future generations might more abundantly live. These places embody holy ground where past hatred has become present love, where death has become life, and where pain has become joy.

I hold within my heart a sacred space. It is a personal holy altar where forgiveness has freed me from a personal prison. It is a place where pain has been released through love, and where anguish has relented to peace. For too long I have denied love by holding pain too close to my heart. At such times, fear grasps my soul shutting out all light. Darkness consumes my very being until I lose all desire to continue. There are no great works offered here, just a long series of small deeds performed with great love. My holy ground has no social significance, no cultural importance, and no humanitarian consequence. My holy ground is merely the denial of self-pity, where I release my feelings of victimization, and place my pride on the altar of humility. In so doing I deliberately resolve to submit willingly, meekly, and cheerfully to the will of a Higher Power. This is just a simple shift in values by walking away from self inflicted punishment, and taking responsibility for actions and events. As I approach this sacred space today, my eyes moisten and old feelings return. I recall with humility the moment when I surrendered my will and forgave unconditionally.

* * * * *

11. BURNT TOAST

Who do you know that eats burnt toast? What do you do with life's bread crusts? How about the odds and ends, and the table scraps? Where do those pieces end up, that for one reason or another, aren't as desirable? Everyone wants the best, but then what do we do with the leftovers?

My mother was a "burnt toast" woman. For as long as I can remember, she had the darkest piece on her plate. At times she went to elaborate lengths to scrape off the black crumbs before eating the toast. None of us wanted these scorched pieces, and I guess because of her Depression era perspective, she just didn't want anything wasted. In my youth, I truly thought she actually preferred the burn toast. As I matured, I realized that my mother was saving the best things for us kids. She didn't particularly like the burnt toast, she was just too frugal to throw it out, and because no one else would eat it, she did.

I caught myself eating burnt toast the other day; in fact as a parent I consumed quite a lot of burnt toast. The "Burnt Toast Syndrome" starts out with good intentions. It involves a giving attitude and is sacrificial in nature. These offerings, although small, are genuine and do make it nicer for others, but there is a down side to this burnt toast perspective. Over time, the giver begins to feel unworthy of better things. The long-term effect of settling for second-best is the limiting of personal vision and potential. Consistently denying myself of personal gratification results in a distorted perception. Perhaps labeling myself as undeserving, crosses the line of healthy self image. I'm not advocating uncontrolled decadence here, just a little time for personal care and maintenance. Every once in a while, allowing yourself to enjoy something special, something good, or something nice really does rehabilitate a bruised image. I guess another option is to just be more careful when making the toast in the first place. Now there's a novel thought!

* * * * *

12. ON FORGIVENESS

Driven by difficult personal events, I've made an observation that forgiveness, on a good day, is difficult. It represents the ultimate confrontation with pride when the ego has dug in deep and firm. At this point, justification is running wild, providing the ideal setting for re-injury, compounded misunderstanding, and increased hurt.

The motivation to forgive starts with the offended. But wait! Generally, both sides are offended. So, one side, in a temporary state of weakness, drops personal pride for a moment and allows insight into situations previously unseen. The resulting perspective shines new light on events in question, revealing a degree of liability rejected in past reflections. New insights unveil increased understanding of actions and words. Once seen, sorrow follows, leading to various forms of meditation and resolution. Events aren't forgotten, but they are recast and remembered more accurately. Instead of re-living distortions resulting in re-injury, emotional healing begins. This is a beautiful process which is divine in nature, cleansing in process, and healing in practice. It leads to personal peace.

But, what about the forgiven? What about the other players in this drama? What about those whose actions, words, and deeds of the other that combined with yours to create this environment of mutual hurt and pain? Rejection, misunderstanding, and insult compound over time as both parties endlessly relive their own hurts, creating emotional calluses. How do these souls react to your breakthrough? Do they instantly respond? Do their walls of pain melt like ice in a desert sun? Is their desire to forgive equally as strong, and can it be released through your change of perspective? No. Unfortunately, forgiveness is not reciprocal. Nothing is that simple. The forgiveness breakthrough is personal and partial at best. It is not an all-at-once process, but rather it is progressive, additive, and slow. With time and repeated interactions, security is validated. Even those with willing hearts and mutual desires can be blinded by ego and shackled by pride. Impatience can and will ensure re-injury and hardening. Rejection is excruciating and plays directly to the fears of the ego. Vulnerability and sensitivity are heightened, and expectations exceed reality. If not handled with care, the end can be worse than the start. Forgiveness is about pride and ego. Admitting faults goes in direct opposition to these two. Concerned over image and personal versions of the truth, the ego lives to justify its selective version of reality.

So what is to be done? Simply put, words in kindness are needed. Sincerely, we must ask for forgiveness, knowing that it most likely won't be reciprocated. This must be followed by a lifetime of changed actions and behaviors, with no expectations of reciprocal self-leveling. The truth may in fact remain lost in a sea of mutual distortions and self-preservation. Forgiveness is self-centered. It's about you letting go and terminating your ego's desire for retaliation. It is freeing energy for better uses. Forgiveness is about personal health and increased joy, resulting in peace of mind. It's not about convincing, persuading, justifying, or validating expectations, for such will guarantee disaster. Forgiveness is for you. Expectations of reciprocal enlightenment and emotional openness will ensure failure. The forgiven are free to choose their response. Time is the key, and time cannot be forced. Holding firm to initial forgiveness after repeated rejection isn't easy, but it is essential.

* * * * *

13. PRIDE OF VICTORY

There is no glory in winning. There is no pride as the victor. There is no honor to the conqueror. There are no spoils to be had. The battle should never have happened. The war should never have been waged. Options should never have been forced, minds manipulated, and words uttered in anger. The momentary thrill of the fight is quickly lost to the anguish of the battlefield, strewn with lifeless corpses from both sides. The true costs of the war will never be completely tallied. The scars are eternal, and often not mendable. The great opponent now lies broken. Sadness falls over the scene. The heart begins to feel the hurt that abounds in every direction. Remorse fills the soul. I confess my pride. I plead with every fiber of my being for forgiveness. Not for petty failings or shortcomings, not for unclean acts or thoughts; not for neglected sins of omission, but rather I cry for forgiveness for the broken homes, broken hearts, broken trusts, broken promises, and broken commitments. The gravity of pain is in direct proportion to the ability to restore. Much of the collateral damage on this scene remains unaccounted. It's not about forgetting. Left without remembrance, history does repeat. The desired peace of forgiveness is illusive. True forgiveness lies only with recognition, sorrow, guilt, suffering, and a lot of service. Unconditional charity, not only to the injured but to all who pass, is required. In time, a feeling of comfort appears. Peace begins to settle over the field. Defensiveness and justification are gone, and a clear recollection of personal action and word are vivid. You have no one to forgive until you realize that you do.

* * * * *

14. LET IT GO

Forgiveness is a strange topic. Most often addressed when speaking of others, my thoughts here center on self. The trigger to the entire process begins with an offense. Typically actions or words negatively impact us and offense is taken. This begins a strange process of reciprocal offense leading to exponentially increasing insult, hurt, and retaliation. As the cycle repeats itself, the negative energy grows. It is often never truly known when "first blood" occurred, and many times it wasn't intentional. But, regardless of the cause, the fallout is the same: injured feelings, damaged relationships, and blemished reputations. Left unchecked, an all-consuming disbursement of destructive energy is committed, engulfing all involved. In order to stop the cycle, we are encouraged to step aside from the immediate hurt, set aside anger and disappointment, and let go of resentment from the perceived loss. Only then are we freed from the consuming anger, disappointment, and antagonism.

To forgive another requires stepping back, accepting some liability in the situation, and resolving to let it go. Only then can we be free of the anger, disappointment, and bitterness associated with the alleged event. To forgive an offender frees us from the negative and allows the energy to be allocated in positive, constructive pursuits. A great burden is lifted from our shoulders with the very act. Forgiveness is not forgetting. Without an active recollection and remembrance, we often fall into similar traps. This is a healthy, constructive remembrance ensuring that the situation will not repeat.

* * * * *

15. MISHAPS

As we journey through life, offenses happen both in bound as well as out. Interactions with other travelers lead to mishaps, where some are intentional, but most are not. No one likes an accident. It takes an already busy schedule and sets it back hours or even days. There are personalities who enjoy confrontation, but even they avoid major collisions. At the end of the day I don't believe anyone enjoys arguing and the hurt feelings and broken relationships that follow. Once an incident has occurred and damage ensued, what then? How do we attend to the wound? Hurt is like infection that, when left unattended, will grow and spread, negatively affecting all precious flesh in its path.

* * * * *

16. I'M SORRY

Recently it was brought to my attention by someone I dearly love, that I had never said that I was sorry for an incident which occurred many months prior and had involved all who were dear to me. This incident derailed many lives, and even now the wounds, although healing, are concealing eternal damage. Quite frankly I was shocked, for in reality I felt that I was the victim and that the apology was due me and not the reverse.

After pondering the topic for a time, the following thesis developed. I concluded that what everyone is striving for is forgiveness. This must be more than just words. It must include a profound sense of cleansing that is possible only after great sorrow on the part of all involved. With that perspective in mind, the myriad of possible actions or reactions can then be placed in context. Sorrow and hurt result in guilt and blame. No one is blameless in a conflict of relationships. Offense, either perceived or real, originates somewhere. Whether it occurred in real time or as the result of festering, hurts don't happen in a vacuum. Even the immediate aggression of one party is most likely a delayed reaction to a past perception. Until sorrow for the damaged relationship is genuinely felt, nothing moves. Self-pity locks up the action. Once a party feels sorrow, the urge to confess can surface. Regret prematurely delivered in the rebuilding process, will muddy the water and confuse the issue. Too much detail can actually set the relationship back, not forward. Even the offering of forgiveness appears judgmental and condescending at the early stages.

What about an apology, stated simply, quietly, and sincerely? Not an acceptance of all responsibility and guilt, just a simple statement of sadness for the loss of, or damage to, the relationship. Admitting pain for your part of the conflict and sorrow for the hurt inflicted is needed. This is always appropriate as it validates genuineness, and shows maturity and humility. In time, the offering of forgiveness comes naturally, but only after sufficient mending has resulted. Ultimately the sense of being forgiven is felt. This feeling comes independent of anyone involved, for it is based on a grander scheme and a grander sacrifice. The feeling of peace comes in due time as a replacement for the anxiety, animosity, and anger, as well as the hurt, sadness, and rage. In the long run it's well worth the wait!

* * * * *

17. THE TESTAMENT

I have a good friend who has become highly successful financially and socially. A few years back he was building a new home on many acres, with many rooms, and lots of neat stuff. One day as we were catching up, my friend started talking about his dad who was a successful man in every way, but more importantly he was a very kind and gentle man, a gentleman's gentleman and definitely a role model to me.

During the process of building his new home this friend's dad had a habit of showing up on site and collecting all the bent nails. In addition, he would gather all the scraps of fine wood which were lying around. The wood made sense because of its quality and value, perfect for small projects. But, why collect the bent nails? Was he trying to make the work site safe? Was he just helping out? Was he just bored? No, he was taking them home and straightening them out. Why, I wondered, would he expend so much effort and energy to complete a task when the price of a pound of any size nail was just a few dollars, and they were already straight and strong?

Having grown his company to an industry leader, this friend was obviously in a position to buy his dad millions of fine straight nails, and just as many board feet of the world's finest lumber. Well as it turns out, this friend's dad had lived his youth during the Great Depression and he intimately understood the notion of value and scarcity. Back then, nails were a great commodity. Not only were nails expensive, but they were not readily available. His conservative nature was established in his youth and his subsequent successes were obviously a by-product of such frugality. He was prudent, humble, honest, and grateful.

While visiting with this friend's dad many months later, the conversation turned to the "big house." We talked of the size, we talked of the quality, we talked of the view, and we talked of the cost. There was a pause in the conversation and then this friend's dad stated without hesitation, "He'll never get more than 50 cents on the dollar when he sells it." My puzzled look triggered an additional utterance, "It's just a testament to himself."

WOW! A stronger sermon I have never experienced. How often are our works, sacrifices, and performances in reality just “testaments to ourselves?”

* * * * *

18. HAPPILY EVER AFTER

Happiness, happiness, oh, happiness. That fickle, fleeting, self-centered emotion. "I just want to be happy, is that asking so much?" Happy is an emotion, and at best, emotions are appreciation for, or linked to, entertainment.

Think deeply for a moment about your personal experience with happiness. It either hasn't happened or it hasn't lasted. Why, when referring to happiness in relationships such as husband and wife, parent and child, or romantic committed partners, is it considered an illusion? Is it because the spouse is supposed to be marvelous, the income is supposed to be marvelous, the children are supposed to be marvelous, the home is supposed to be marvelous, and you are supposed to be marvelous? You are not supposed to be depressed. You should not be discouraged, bored, or sad. You should be united in blissful harmony. You should be in love. You should adore your job. You should be happy!

There is a reason why the cover of any typical romance novel pictures a beautiful, buxom woman in front of a dark, deserted castle waiting for the arrival of her handsome prince to rescue her. That's the illusion, and it perpetuates today's discontent. Let's take a look at the classic fairytale princesses. All of these wretched beauties are pink, perky, sparkling, and obsessed with fashion. They are all preoccupied with their bodies, their beauty, and the cleanliness of their homes. All, unfortunately, are extremely passive in life, and personally helpless on their own. Without a prince to bring them true love and so deliver them from their painful lives, they are left alone to cry.

First in the line of fairytale beauties is Snow White. So patiently she waits day after day to be made happy. "Some day my Prince will come." Oh please, give me a bucket! It is interesting to note that the prince doesn't arrive until he is darn good and ready. Then there is Cinderella. The poor girl is battered and abused, and helplessly waiting for emancipation. Waiting, suffering, and serving, she patiently passes the time until the Fairy Godmother fixes family injustices so that the prince will then select her as his bride. They also throw in a lot of cute mice for distraction and entertainment. We can't bypass Sleeping Beauty. Due to her overwhelming beauty, she is poisoned by family. Quietly, patiently, beautifully, and with perfect hair, she waits until her prince arrives. Again he arrives on his timetable and at his good pleasure. He finally delivers the kiss that awakens her from the numbing, listless sleep which has kept her bound. And, what about Rapunzel? She's not doing a darn thing but growing perfect hair and waiting, waiting, waiting, for a perfect prince to rescue her. Wouldn't it be cool if that were all it took to be happy: perfect guy, with perfect finances, with a perfect kiss, not to mention great hair. That retched habit of romance. This type of victim-like thinking is perilous on the mental and physical health of little girls. This kind of thinking hammers into young girls that it's better to be married than to be successful, accomplished, or content.

Feelings like pleasure and happiness create a high, but they never remain strong. These natural barriers and limits create tension, anxiety, fear, doubt, and distrust. This special tension is an uncomfortable strain, and an unhappy pressure. This is where the ego enters in, adjusting personal perspective, and making things happy again. When we become dependent upon the ego's magic, we lose ownership of our lives.

Other kinds of highs are tied to personal accomplishments through career and physical attainment. All are dependent and unpredictable. Highs fade regardless of their development; that's just a fact. You eventually get to know the guy and he becomes predictable. You begin to feel overly secure or overly insecure with the relationship. Emotions just fade over time. The myth concerning happiness, pleasure, infatuation, exhilaration, and passion is that these will endlessly last. But, in reality, emotions fade. That's just how it is, and so eventually there you are wondering where your "happy" went? It's difficult to think objectively concerning feelings and not let emotions dominate when you are carried away in the quest for happy.

Some people are only happy when in love or caught up in the heat of romance. That retched habit of romance damages many a good life through attendant discontent. Being emotionally high is not reality, not normal, and should not be expected. The opposite of happy is a feeling of the blues, or an emotional low. Everyone has as many of one as the other. Some people live in a world of extreme highs and extreme lows: way up and way down. You know these people because they are always halfway to the moon or halfway to committing suicide. These very dramatic souls are emotionally draining to all who love them. The higher the ball bounces the harder it hits the ground. Most healthy people reside in the middle of the road striving to be content and comfortable.

A trap of the emotional extreme is the "if only" reaction. There is no such thing as "if only." You are not supposed to be happy all the time. The Fairy Godmother syndrome states, "If only… looks, weight, actions were a little better, my prince would rescue me." She with her little wand promises to makes everything better with a simple touch. The magic of the Fairy Godmother promises happiness ever after! But, the reality is that happiness is the mortar keeping the bricks of life securely in place. All mortar and all buildings can fail in time.

Sooner or later you need to think about your personal capacity and ability. Think objectively and don't let emotions dominate. Stop thinking of self in terms of happiness, for this is arrogance. The person who controls your life, controls your happiness. Illusions and fantasy are arrogance.

Happiness is grounded in the emotional, and is based upon arrogance. As such, it must be controlled and disciplined. What we think is what we seek. Humility and arrogance are mutually exclusive. Humility is the basis for virtue. Humility is not innate. Humility must be learned. In a state of humility you can get along with anyone. Without genuine humility you can never be content. Humility recognizes authority and requires submission.

* * * * *

19. PINE

There, alongside a heavily traveled trail in the woods near Sun Valley, Idaho, stands a mighty pine, distinctive from all around it. It represents a unique life lived in spite of similar circumstances to its sister pines. By trunk width, it is one of the largest around, a testament to its ability to survive and endure nature's challenges. Shorter than many of its peers, it has compensated by the breadth of its canopy. Upon closer glance it is discovered that five distinct trunks have formed about 10 feet above the ground, protruding horizontally at first, and then abruptly all advance vertically. Enormous masses initially entangled in confusion, these trunks unite to eventually stretch skyward. Deep within the center of the entanglement stands what is left of the original trunk, that is now withered, gray, cracked, and dead.

Conifers such as this grow a canopy in direct proportion to their tap root, a mirror image to the height of the growth above. So what happened so many years ago, I wonder, which nearly terminated this tree's existence? Was there one single event which was so profound that it radically changed its genetic nature? It appears that shortly after this fundamental event, a choice was presented for the pine to either adapt and grow, or to wither and die. Somehow this mighty pine found the determination to survive. Slow at first, but with increasing momentum until now, it stands as a testament to those sensitive enough to see it for what it is: a monument of courage in the midst of catastrophe. Surely it would have been easier to give up, shrivel, and die. Surely this path of acquiescence was justified, given the magnitude of the incident and the probability of failure. At best, the pine would be different. Never again to be as the others, not now, not after this. The course was permanently altered. Why try? Why continue when original objectives and dreams were now beyond reach? What transpired within this majestic pine to determine its course to carry on in spite of the challenges? What was the source of courage inspiring it to become the best it could be in spite of this handicap? What sustained it in the early stages of growth, when just surviving required all the energy available? And, so here it stands as a testament to all who have an eye to see. Its beauty lies not in statistics, but in majesty and uniqueness, truly "one of a kind."

All of us confront challenges and events of life-changing proportion. All of us lose hope and desire. All of us get discouraged, disappointed, and depressed. Our futures are not determined by these incidents. Our futures are determined, as with the pine, by our response to these defining moments. It takes immeasurable courage to emerge a mighty pine in the forests of life. What is the magnitude of courage you will need to display to adapt and grow in the storms of your life?

* * * * *

20. LIFT-OFF

Billions of man-hours were committed to build and maintain the 2.5 million components required to fly the U.S. space shuttle. This is the most complex machine yet created by man. Eighty-three percent of the thrust required to enter hypersonic orbital flight is utilized to break the hold of gravity. Six million pounds-force of thrust is consumed in the first two minutes of lift off. Once beyond subsonic atmospheric flight, little energy is required to maneuver and relocate at the orbital level. It is during two critical minutes of lift off that laser-like focus and energy is required for success. Any momentary flaw or hesitation, as with the Challenger in 1986, will send the entire ship to the earth in total ruin. Not just a return to the safety of the launch pad to regroup, but instead hurling to the surface in total destruction. This is an all or nothing deal. Extensive tests and calculations were required to refine and perfect the propulsion principals. Hours of design were required to validate thrust, duration, and processes, but it isn't until actual flight that success is determined.

No wonder most of us choose to remain safe and secure in our protected little worlds, assured by the fact that our neighbors are also pacified as each in turn reinforces the other. So many of us focus on the building rather than the living; we are overcome in the planning instead of the actual journey. So few of us ever experience true "lift off."

Recently, I found myself wallowing in regret, and desperately struggling to return to safety. As with the shuttle, transitioning between the earth and the heavens is no easy task. The contentment and satisfaction of peer approval, the pleasure and happiness of the immediate, and the momentary gratification and enjoyment of indulgence and self-absorption easily distract me from my true goal. These strong emotions become the chains of gravity that tether me to the temporal.

It's interesting that this refining process of "lift off" requires great courage, self-determination, commitment, and intelligence, but once developed or attained you must submit to meekness. This is no easy task because the rewarded traits of our current existence are counter-productive and oppressive to submission. True submission is not a partial wiggling between pride and humility. It is not a weekly gesture overshadowed by faint performance. Once truly committed, you cannot look back because momentary doubt, just like a weak component in space shuttle design, can lead to total failure. Future malfunctions can be tolerated when in orbit. Then there is time for personal improvement and refinement of thought. It's during the initial thrust when breaking gravity that we must be focused, steady, and sure.

So why do we continue to look back? Why do we hesitate? Is it fear, embarrassment, doubt, greed, or pride? Do we lack commitment and a depth of understanding? Do we become so caught up in the gravitational pull of the temporal that we unintentionally sacrifice the liberating power of the heavens? This "take off" requires more than token offerings, more than momentary valor, and more than transitory discomfort. For success, all temporal securities must be consecrated to the attainment of personal humility. Comfort and contentment must be offered upon the altar of submission. Then and only then will the temporal diminish in importance. Then and only then will attention and desire shift to the well being of others. Then and only then will we be provided with worldly needs beyond our ability to perceive them. This will occur not as we currently desire but in direct proportion to our change of heart.

The sad reality is that few people really want to "take off" to the moon. Most of us are content to labor diligently in readying the ship.

* * * * *

21. I AM THE SCULPTOR

Occasionally in our lives we are forced to take a good look at our inner self. In these quiet moments, we have the opportunity to reflect on who we really are. Such moments come in the hurried flow of events when obligations to look deeply beyond the obvious are easily overlooked. Time, quiet time, unhurried time, alone time, is what is needed. Time is needed to ponder reality as compared to perceived self-images. Seldom do these two align naturally on their own. More often, it is an event which propels us towards such reflective thoughts.

As we mingle with our fellow travelers, most of us choose to select the elements and observations which reinforce our current sense of identity. This doesn't ensure that the image is accurate. In fact, many of us selectively choose only the feedback that reinforces our sacred self-perception. Occasionally we get the uncomfortable glimpse of our true self. Often this isn't as flattering as the illusion. Self-preservation motivates us to reject this as impossible, even offensive. "This couldn't be a part of ME!" Isn't it curious how hard we defend the illusions, when accepting the possibility of flaws would actually free us from the bondage of self-deception, and thereby provide an opportunity for growth. Are we all so insecure that the slightest negative feedback is immediately taken as a personal attack rather than as a blessing for personal growth? We can't and shouldn't listen to everything thrown our way, positive or negative, but feedback should be viewed as an opportunity to adjust our paradigms as needed.

Many make a living feeding on the souls of innocent bystanders through put-downs devised to elevate the giver. A healthy awareness of self states that I, in reality, may be flawed. and that I may, in truth, not come across as I perceive. During these times of quiet reflection, as actuality bombards the imaginary, a choice is placed before us. We can reject the new perspective as a cruel and undeserved observation and thus blindly proceed along in the illusion, or we can or accept the possibility that the new feedback may hold some truth. We can courageously choose to view this as a small key which unlocks significant opportunity for change and improvement. This latter option inspires growth, refinement, and fulfillment. The embarrassment over past follies is quickly offset by the comfort of future performance.

I am the sculptor. I am the clay. Each cut removes precious flesh. Each cut inflicts pain. Each cut brings me that much closer to my destiny. This process of self evaluation takes courage, but without this brutally painful process, I will never become the master of myself, I will never become the sculptor of my own fate, and I will never become the masterpiece of my vision.

* * * * *

22. REVEALED

Walls are built to provide safety and protection against outside forces. When we build protective walls around ourselves, the forces that seek to break through our barriers are all the vulnerabilities and insecurities accumulated over time. They include the insults and misjudgments from others that causes hurt and mistrust. A wall should fortify me against the barrage of such attacks.

Feeling vulnerable is a byproduct of new situations, and this is often a time when we seek safety behind the protective walls we have built. The unknown and the uncertain seem to heighten my sensitivities to the point of overload. During such times, I become easily wounded and easily hurt. Normal communications can be perceived as criticisms or attack. Feelings of "fight or flight" prevail. It takes courage to get beyond the safety of my protective wall where I am exposed to all. To protect myself, I fortify the existing walls that insulate and cover my delicate, susceptible self. Sensing threat, discomfort, embarrassment, or intimidation, this strong barrier calls out a defense in the form of defiance, humor, sarcasm, paranoia, or anger. This wall is to provide safety and security to the true me, the part that no one sees. If anyone had access beyond this wall I would be revealed, and so all my weaknesses and shortcomings are buried behind it. Over time these flaws become bigger than life, and detailed beyond reason. From back here my true thoughts, my behaviors, and my actions are regulated. I may speak with the tongue of a lion, but behind the wall, and in face-to-face situations, I am exposed. My courage, my success, and my confidence is predicated on perceptions of past interactions. The number of times, the depth of openness, and the ultimate outcomes of the interface all regulate my next engagement. Vulnerability arises with each new incident, but today, with confidence and resolve, I will allow the unknown ship to draw near. I will defy my own resistance and open the gate allowing entrance into my private space. Occasionally I will misread interactions and pain might be experienced again. Is the risk worth the reward? Behind my wall I am safe. Over time I will mend and grow strong. With courage I will begin to fulfill my purpose. Can I learn to live outside the walls that hold me hostage to my insecurities? I will trust. Eventually I can break the protective walls. Little successes are experienced as I courageously face my real self.

23. THE COURAGE TO OVERCOME

As human beings, we are pain avoidant by nature. The majority of our lives are spent either directly going around "it," or developing and preparing plans to ensure we don't have to endure "it." We consume our hours and days developing financial security so as to provide ourselves with stable, happy lives void of discomfort and trauma. The stronger our financial position, the smoother life can be. Given enough money and time, most situations can be avoided or resolved without emotion. Sorrow can be soothed, pain anesthetized, and disappointment and hurt avoided. But, what happens if these vibrant human emotions and feelings are critical to our individual growth? What if the abilities and maturity gained in struggling, wrestling, and fighting, are only achieved in the "valley of despair?" What if the easy way, the smooth way, the direct way isn't the right way? If certain attitudes, abilities, and experiences can only develop as part of emotional devastation, a great loss is experienced in their avoidance. I'm not advocating a life in pursuit of trials, but merely one of accepting, with a bright heart, the challenges confronted. The time will come when each of us will meet trials and hardships. The time will come when we will not be able to rely on borrowed light. By seeing these trials as an opportunity to grow and overcome, strength is born in the heart and spirit. Cowardice is a byproduct of avoiding duty, responsibility, or opportunity. At the end of the day, we are left with our individual spirit and soul, which is the sum total of our experiences both happy and sad. At such times, possessions will vanish, positions will disappear, appearances will fade, inheritances will end, and relationships will fade. It's just me and the mirror. The cold reality of what I have become is all that is left. There will be no excuses, no scapegoats, and no justifications. At such times, I must ask myself, "Am I everything I was destined to be?" In reflecting on the reality of being human, I commit now to weather the storms of life. When fears and challenges knock on my door threatening to "blow my house down," I commit to accept them, to struggle with them, and to learn from them.

There will always be those who feel most comfortable not venturing from the warmth and security of home and hearth. Adventurous thoughts arise, but will be set aside before they can take root. But, hidden deep within the cracks and corners of life are those who prefer to look out the window and wonder what is beyond the horizon. The easiest choices in life just aren't all that fun or interesting. Our practical voice encourages us to let the new idea go. But the other voice, the venturesome, the irresponsible, the passionate voice says, "Go for it!" Even if the path leads you down a back alley in the center of nowhere in the middle of the night, with no immediate meaning, then sit back and enjoy the ride. The courageous voice of the inner child tells us that when we leap, the net will appear.

* * * * *

24. THE RUNNER STUMBLES

Trained, conditioned, poised, and ready in every way, the starting gun releases a massive surge of kinetic energy as runners unleash the power within. The body explodes into action as adrenaline instantly floods into every filament. "This is what I've been training for. This is what I've been waiting for. This is what I was made for!" The time is NOW! This is a defining moment of my life. Muscles warm as they find their stride. The mind, now laser-focused, blocks all outside thoughts and distractions. One goal remains; one objective; one mission: I will finish. I will succeed. I will win! For a brief moment the entire grand plan appears in magnificent context of this defining race. But, it can vanish as quickly as it came through one millisecond of doubt. What if?

Surrounded by beautiful specimens whose bodies gleam from the sweat of motion, I think to myself, "What indescribable joy to be part of the whole." At the top of my game, I have prepared, I have trained, and I have conditioned for this moment. Truly it is the climax of my thoughts and habits in the exhausting and extensive preparation I have done. I quickly find my pace as I settle into the routine. I am painfully aware of the entire process, having rehearsed it for decades. "Enjoy this moment," I recall hearing, "for all too soon it is replaced with the fatigue and pain attendant to all long distance races."

A glimpse of doubt again attempts to slither into my thoughts, but it vanishes as I round the first turn. A quick glance at my immediate challengers reveals an unanticipated contender. Unnoticed in the preliminary events due to his unassuming size and stature, he surprises me as I'm shuffled to the edge in this mass of competitors. "What's this about?" Nothing in his demeanor prepared me for this: shorter stride, smaller muscle mass, and void of the "winners" air. My premature judgment lacked the insight of his "on-track" ability. No poetry here, for what he lacked in power and grace, he made up for in drive and determination, combined with the synergy of motion. Everything about him now seemed to unite in a powerful force propelling him forward. Without thought, I responded with increased pace and longer stride, confidently leaving him behind. That accomplished, I again re-focused upon my game. "This is THE race of my existence, my moment; there is no margin for error." I know the drill, and anything short of perfection is unacceptable. There will be plenty of time for reflection after the victory. For now I must remain on task as success is not assured until the end. Run true, run strong, run hard, run smart, and WIN! I can't afford to lose focus.

Mentally back on track, I again feel the familiar sensation of being "on my game." All fibers of my being combine to one simple objective: optimized motion. This is similar to the first act of a play. After being rehearsed to internalization, the gratification of the actual performance validates the sacrifice. Back on track and in my groove, the laps now pass. First one, then a second, and soon a blur as time advances me along my predetermined path, ever closer to my determined objective. Well into the heat now, I begin to feel the fatigue of it all. All runners know that the race doesn't necessarily go to the strongest, the fastest, or to the brightest. Victory is dependent upon discipline, commitment, and focus leading to completion. Energy management weighs equally with actual quantity and quality. Enduring is every bit as important as maintaining lead position. The key is knowing the exact moment to release the reserved kick when all are tired, when all are fatigued, when muscles burn, when energy levels are depleted, and when stamina falters. This is where the victory is determined.

Each of us here on this race is equally prepared physically. Now it comes down to a mind game. This is where I am now. Caught off guard by the actual pressure of reality, nothing could have prepared me for this. A quick glance around assesses the relative condition of my peers. I am not alone in my state; in fact many appear to be fairing even worse. Again I snap back to reality and the task at hand. While assessment is valuable it is also distracting and can prove counterproductive if done to excess. For now I know that I must focus all my efforts to the last great kick. This is my "defining moment."

As I kick into the final leg, a new found energy emerges. Muscles, bone, and sinew merge and tighten as lungs supply the vital supply to heart and soul. I am "on-fire" as every element of my being is working to one end. I feel truly alive with feet barely touching the earth as I glide toward my goal. I can actually taste my victory now. Suddenly, without notice, my thoughts of victory are disrupted by a sense of disorder. "This isn't right! It can't possibly be!" A simple misplaced step has thrown everything out of order. Struggling to regain control, individual components begin reacting to one another reducing themselves to chaos. What once was so sublime has in an instant become bedlam. As each muscle wrestles to regain composure, the problem compounds exponentially and the original incident is exacerbated. My mind now races to make sense of it all. Instead of victory, confusion. Instead of warmth, pain. Instead of air, dust. I tumble helplessly to the ground. My worst nightmare materializes as I lay motionless on the track. Struggling to regain composure, I sense the passing of others more fortunate than myself. Victory is gone in a moment. From "winner" to loser" in an instant. All of my hopes, aspirations, and expectations crash with me. As my body comes to rest in the dirt, I scream in agony and self pity, "What NOW!" The last competitor passes my tormented form and all I can do is ask, "Why ME? How did this happen? Whose fault was it? Did someone push me?" My worst nightmare is now fulfilled. "Did I not prepare adequately? Was I not conditioned sufficiently? Did I lack focus for a moment?" Equipped in every way, it was not conditioning or fault, I conclude. Could it have possibly been the increased pressure of the actual event, or the unanticipated distraction of the unforeseen challenger? Yes, that was it. He threw me off my game, expelling needed reserves, and prematurely leaving me vulnerable and exposed. "But what now?" I face a challenge unimagined and unprepared for. Possibly it is the greatest challenge of my existence to date. Victory is now a fleeting imagination, and success is lost instantly. Even acceptable placement in the race is unattainable. Now what?

Mid thought, I feel my body begin to arise. Against the will of a battered ego, I find myself standing erect again. Blood now replaces sweat, and mud packed sores dominate a once glistening physique. Soon conscious thoughts catch up to my inner being. Endurance, completion, and finishing emerge as the sole objective. "I will succeed." Alone, on the course, my soiled soul begins to regain its life force.

As I near the finish line I become aware of the roar of the crowd as the significance of my behavior is placed in context of the grander test. We have all been part of a grander competition. Not competitor poised against one another, but rather a struggle against self. This "battle with self" is determined only after pushed beyond capacity, beyond ability, and beyond reason. Only then can true character be measured and recorded for eternity.

As I cross the line, ultimate joy consumes my soul beyond anything anticipated or imagined. My unforeseen victory outshines perceptions, as does my reward. To win is certainly grand, to achieve is supreme, but to find the courage to endure, yes, endure to the end, this is timeless!

* * * * *

25. RATIONALIZATIONS

The act of easing one's conscience by excusing questionable behavior as being justified, condoned, or the exception, is something of which we all are guilty. These rationalizations contain a portion of truth, making them easy to believe and embrace. We scream to ourselves, "My behavior is the exception to the rule because of extenuating circumstances beyond my control." Driven by personal agendas, it is easy to believe the logic of our rationalized arguments. But, at the end of the day, the degree of our distortions account for the extent of inaccuracy in our position. I think they call that delusional. Even with extensive promotion of our perspective to significant others, leading to mutual consent, errors in judgment that are left unresolved, will remain etched in our being. These fatal flaws break our arguments under intense scrutiny and pressure. Only visible when pressed, these rationalizations will remain unexposed until pressures and stresses build to volcanic proportions.

How can we recognize our own deceptions? How can we uncover our deadly flaws? How can we identify personal inaccuracies in perception? Only those with courage to face the molten lava flow within can contain emotional eruptions. Without painful reflection initiated by profound events that challenge our very purpose, we will not see and we will not control. Blinded to imperfections that alter perspectives, we see ourselves only to the degree needed to justify our behavior. Caught in reality we choose to blame and justify, or to accept, internalize, and improve.

Today I will choose to accept this truth and in so doing internalize it. I may not see all my shortcomings, but at least some. I cannot do it all now, but at least it's a start. I've taken the first step; the age of innocence is over. I can never return to illusions of the past, and surprisingly, I can live with that. Pride is felt, not for past behavior, but for accepting the correction without further rationalization.

* * * * *

28. UNCERTAINTY

We all need, but none of us enjoys, uncertainty for the future. It's said that if we follow the promptings of our inner soul we will be directed regardless of the events confronted. What does this actually mean? This positive affirmation translates into "Don't be afraid; don't give up; don't be sad." Laugh with children, be cheerful, be comforted, and be positive. Read, ponder, be obedient, and express gentle, genuine love to all, even the unlovable. Live as if things are fine, and they will be.

Perspective is the key, isn't it? Short views and limited vision regarding the proceedings of this mortal life, quickly lead to the unbearable. All events, desperate and destructive, will turn beneficial in time. Given an eternal perspective, all events will ultimately lead to growth. Remember, most beef is tough, most jobs are frustrating, most marriages are challenged, and most kids disappoint. Throughout the mundane miles of the journey, grab hold of the vistas and relish them. Life is truly a test, and many events just need to be endured. It is not a pleasure cruise. We are not forgotten. I believe that our journey is custom tailored to maximize personal growth and development. Everything endured builds tolerance, character, maturity, and tenderness. The crucible, if used as a device for refinement, is useless without heat.

Cheerful insecurity seems to sum it up quite well. Due to our limited mental capacity, diminished perspective, and personal doubt, we are all insecure. But just because everything experienced is not understood does not mean that it is out of control. Cheerful insecurity suggests that plans of a Higher Power are not fully revealed, nor immediately comprehended. In time, this insecurity leads to security, this doubt leads to belief, and this desperation leads to jubilation. This fear, this uncertainty, leads to peace. Time is the key.

* * * * *

27. STICKY FINGERPRINTS

Impressions left in stone reveal the presence of past visitors. The sensation of a touch can be recalled years later. Like my grandson's sticky fingerprints on the glass tabletop, my life is covered with unique impressions etched upon my soul for eternity. The book of life is written in our very souls, engraved upon bone and sinew. All thoughts, words, and deeds leave marks. The body's conformance to timeless laws either leaves it clean, pure, and spotless, or decayed, distorted, and incomplete. When the book of life is opened, our bodies will reveal the virtues we have valued. These virtues enable us to live timeless laws that result in peaceable lives even while existing in a world of decay and corruption. Insulated from the poisons, distractions, and temptations around us, the virtues etched in our souls can sustain us when we fall short. Each of us is individually, intimately, and independently accountable for our ultimate state and condition. The eventual degree of joy received is in direct proportion to the demonstrated capacity developed.

Sometimes we may need to clean those sticky fingerprints from our tabletops as we seek to refresh and revitalize our lives.

* * * * *

28. CLEANLINESS IS CONTROL

The body is an unreliable friend. We see ourselves as bundles of flesh and bone which, at best, accommodate a multitude of dichotomies: pleasure and pain, health and sickness, dirty and clean. These opposing experiences are transitory, and must be endured with calmness, while at the same time seeking to gain control of self. Imagination is the door through which disease, as well as healing, enters. Disbelief in the reality of sickness, even when plagued by illness, may cause it to disappear. Many of our challenges are the result of self-fulfilling prophecy. We must cease being a prisoner of the body, and escape to the spirit. Reflect unceasingly, beholding self as an infinite substance free from every misery. Cleanliness of thought is freedom.

What we fail to find within ourselves will not be found traversing the globe. The human eye sees the physical, but the inner eye sees more profoundly. Intuition is soul guidance, appearing naturally in those instants when one's mind is calm. Everyone has had an experience of an unexplainably correct "hunch," or has sensed the familiarity of transferring thoughts accurately to another person. The human mind, freed from the disturbances of restlessness, is empowered to perceive thoughts unimaginable. To calm the mind minimizes distortion so as to hear the unerring advice of the inner voice. Cleanliness is control (Gandhi, 1946).

* * * * *

29. DARKNESS AND LIGHT

There is a dark, primal force inside me that seeks to control all. It feeds on primitive instincts based on carnal and sensual appetites. These personal weaknesses are mine from the beginning. To greater or lesser degrees, all humanity fights this same battle. Dante's seven sins of Pride, Envy, Wrath, Sloth, Greed, Gluttony, and Lust are the byproducts of this dark force, and are incompatible with my desired state of enlightenment.

My sojourn through life has but one purpose: to experience first hand the consequences of my choices. It is not about failure, but about growth; growth over weaknesses not enjoyment with strengths. It is about facing my primitive nature and overcoming the dark by embracing the light. This struggle is a battle of energies. Fear depletes personal energy, and succumbing to passions neutralizes it. Strength comes through good acts of kindness, self-control, and love. The synergistic influence of souls united through respect, wisdom, integrity, and trust is indeed greater than the sum of the individuals. The achievement of individual strength, multiplied through the grouping of equally committed entities, is true power. The resulting exponential force makes each member impervious to darkness. Fear of failure, fear of embarrassment, fear of pain, and fear of weakness relegates the power back. In the battle between darkness and light, power is attained through this band of souls personally committed to the betterment of one another. As charity increases, self diminishes and darkness recedes.

* * * * *

30. SIGNS

The earthen filled dam is a cost effective method of preserving spring runoff for use during the hot summer days. Without it there would be no crops in the deserts of the earth. Relatively inexpensive to build when compared to the over engineered concrete structures which hold back massive river flows, these irrigation reservoirs dot the countryside of the farming communities of the world. Without them there is no agricultural base. Early spring rains sustain the young crops naturally, but just as the peak demand for moisture is reached the rain stops abruptly. Within days the crop is lost to the dry hot sun if not irrigated.

These simple dams are nothing more than a lot of dirt placed in a narrow portion of a stream bed that holds back the spring runoff for later use. The original design was by dumb luck. Failures inspired improvements. Today there are extensive calculations as to how much fill is required to retain a given quantity of water. We're talking millions of cubic feet of water here, the force of which is devastating if released at once. Taking one of the most powerful forces of nature and messing with it isn't a joke. Thousands of lives have been lost along with untold property damage due to the uncontrolled failure of these simple structures. The danger with the earthen filled dam lies in the inability to detect failure in advance. Once moisture is detected on the outer surface it is generally too late.

Water is a strange beast. Slowly and persistently it finds its way through anything. It never sleeps. If it permeates the dirt it is only a matter of time until the very dam saturates, and its restricting power converts to destruction as the structure liquefies. Rushing downstream, this once sturdy structure wipes out everything in its path. Fast and violent, it is over in an instant. Nothing can hold back the energy once it has been released. Just get out of the way! In moments, lives are dramatically changed forever.

History shows that attempts to save the structure are futile once moisture has made it through the mass. The source of the catastrophe lies just beneath the surface. It is real and serious. Once the first signs are detected, the safety and preservation of life is the sole business. The outcome is inevitable: the structure and downstream properties are gone. It's a matter of time. Reading the signs saves lives.

31. SHADES OF GRAY

All of my life I've been taught to avoid evil and hold close to good. In my youth I often generalized about things, which made it easy to label situations as black and white, cold and hot, or light and dark. Since I've grown I discriminate a lot more. Things don't fit into the neat little categories of my childhood. Can mostly good possess some bad? Can evil have an element of light? If one issue is quite dark but it is sitting right on top of an obviously lighter matter and both are interrelated, what then? By changing the context the whole matter gets snarled. I'm drowning in shades of gray. It appears impossible to make sense of the whole matter. Then there is the issue of hue: warm gray as opposed to cold gray. Suppose you have the same tone but different hues; is one better than the other?

Left unattended, my thoughts become skeptical of absolute good in this life. Doesn't this very thought in turn unintentionally support evil? In the midst of this emotional quagmire of color extremes, I must stop and reset my comparisons and my thoughts to that of the pureness of white.

* * * * *

32. TRUE NEEDS

By default, when groups of people gather together, rules, standards, and expectations emerge. For the most part, such rules imposed upon us by society are to keep us safe. They are the agreed upon standards of social decency. I respect you and in turn I expect the same courtesies. Along with the societal rules come collective expectations. Society places great importance and acclaim on the high achiever regardless of the field of endeavor: music, sports, academics, the stage, and so forth. Logically we assume that this societal value system of wealth, notoriety, achievement, and position is valid.

Contrary to societal priorities of right and wrong, the improving of one's position often takes precedence over all. This is where personal pride and esteem dominate will. Developed talents are utilized for gain, not good. Token crumbs of kindness are thrown out to subdue guilt, but they fall radically short of true needs. All are striving for safety, security, and position. All are bequeathed by secular sources. Counterfeit sanctuary in an earthly sea is as good as it gets. But, what of my needs and the needs of loved ones? Do they not constitute true need? The problem appears to be not in the offering itself, but in the intent of the heart. Self determined needs often are not valid. A child makes poor use of power, and vision is short. We, like they, also miss our objective, our potential, and our ordination.

Necessities, like security, are a moving target, often undefined and never truly attainable. Where we invest our most precious commodity, our time, is how we reveal the true motives in our heart. The terminally ill feel no remorse for not spending more time at work. The illusion that more wealth means more freedom for family and others, is as invalid today as it was 2000 years ago. The age old trapping is only broken when we develop the strength to say, "Enough!" I choose to be happy here, now, at this present moment. I have sufficient for my needs. At that moment of personal contentment, the individual is freed to glimpse the plight of others: to be given as I need not as I want, to be content with my position, to be at peace with my life. This position is not to idleness or sloth, but rather a feeling of satisfaction with my purpose, no matter how common. The societal race of bigger, better, faster, and newer will never end. Like raccoons, whose curiosity often traps them, we bore easily and envy much. Discontent is of the world. Eternal wealth is built upon relationships of service, sacrifice, and caring. My true need is to have the ability to love the unlovable, the damaged, and the discarded.

* * * * *

33. OUR HOUSE OF CARDS

I was exposed to the world of cards at a young age. I loved to watch my parents and their friends gather together to play games. I learned the rules of the game, the lingo, the strategies, and the competitive spirit. I learned that one wrong play by a well-intentioned teammate could mean defeat. I learned that to build one's hopes on the flimsy and whimsical nature of a game was foolhardy, as there was always the danger of collapse, of failure, and of personal loss.

I also discovered that a steady hand and keen mind could, in fact, build a structure of walls and floors out of these very cards. As it turns out, once the initial cell is created each additional card adds strength. So it goes with each successive floor until quite an impressive construction is built.

In our world of rapidly changing styles and tastes, we, like the fragile house of cards, are all destined to collapse, to fail, and to become obsolete. To combat this, we create needs where none exists, we generate interest where none resides, and we instill desires where none should be. In so doing, we market the downfall of our very existence. Floor after floor we grow, forgetting the delicate balance required for the first cell. With so many choices, so many options, and so many wants, can any truly be fulfilled?

We have been trained to be a fickle generation; our natures are being exploited and our dissatisfactions continue to grow. Unquenched, our thirsts dominate, and our hungers increase. Struggling for peace, we are caught up in a self-made Hell of appetites and passions. Is the eternal impact of a small offering today to someone in need worth more than millions promised tomorrow? Is the exchange rate different in the hereafter? Is wealth measured by denominations other than money? Is our credit rating based upon measures as yet unseen?

Economically the world marketplace once appeared strong and growing, but it, too, is becoming a delicate house of cards. Previously content, all are now falling prey to the power of the market. Upon close examination I see fragility, vulnerability, and weakness, which, left unattended, will ultimately lead to ruin. Such a delicate balance is our life of ease.

Food, warmth, mobility, and information all flow freely and effortlessly with the promise of unending contentment. The greater our dependence, the more insecure we become. Countries are only as good as the beliefs they commonly hold true. Stocks are only as good as the company of issue. Banks are only as good as their assets in hand. People are only as good as the values practiced. Truly, as Dickens wrote, it is the best of times and the worst of times: an age of wisdom and an age of foolishness.

Meaning lies in people. Security lies in relationships. Peace lies in service. In our temporal house of cards, roofs leak, tires flatten, cloths fade, and people retire. It is the warmth of relationships that grow stronger with age that will fortify our houses against inevitable collapse. Focusing upon the good of others appears to be nothing more than an emotional adjustment. It is a refocusing based upon trust that ultimate joy requires a step into the dark, and that a warm reassuring touch is a promise of positive things to come. Our house of cards is fortified in the belief that delayed gratification will result in a change of heart which is, in fact, the source of personal determination, of contentment, and of peace.

* * * * *

34. THE INSTANT GENERATION

We live in an instant world. Everything is immediate. Enormous sums of money are invested daily to make things ever faster. Leapfrogging the past has become the global obsession: faster cars, faster planes, faster data, and faster burgers. I want it and I want it now! The age of the craftsman has fallen prey to the demands of this time-crazed society.

Likewise, I have always been in a hurry. Ever since I was young I couldn't wait for the next program. An adrenalin junkie, the anticipation drove me to force the time window. Not even done with the current event, I was planning the next. When I pause briefly I can still hear my mother's voice faintly in the distance, "Stop and smell the roses."

Somewhere in this race to nowhere, efficiency must be balanced with effectiveness. What is the objective? What is the purpose? Is it merely faster for faster's sake? My axiom of truth has always been "maximum effect for minimum effort." Is this now starting to crumble? The time saved in this race backfills with other meaningless activities. Soon the purpose becomes obscure to the event. I am beginning to see that going to be going, doing to be doing, having to have, and getting to be getting is not good enough!

When I was young a day was forever. As I have aged, time has exponentially shriveled. Now that I have more behind than in front, weeks, months, and years fly by. Future memories can never overtake the past! An inventory of these precious remembrances leaves a bittersweet sadness for opportunities lost. Not for lost achievement, advancement, or acquisition as in the past, but for precious, unplanned moments of tenderness. Moments which just happened because loved ones were there. Rather than pining about the past or fretting about the loss, I will reset my agenda. I will operationally redefine my objectives. I will rewrite my life's mission statement. What was first has now become last, and out of these small adjustments important moments will emerge.

* * * * *

35. SUBMISSION

My father was a brilliant man who never quite fit in. Part of his creativity was based upon not following the rules. Without medical intervention, he fought cancer for over seven years using personal research and unconventional methods before he ultimately died of heart failure. Even this validated his legacy of defiance: he was unwilling to go with the natural course of things. As you are aware cancer begins when a normal working cell for some unknown reason decides that it no longer wants to function in contribution to the whole. Instead of being a small part of a critical support system, it goes off and builds its own kingdom with completely different rules. The resulting anarchy is malignancy. It's strange that my Dad's distinguishing characteristic in life, symbolized by the disease he carried, became my legacy also.

This inherited nature, combined with the defiant, rebellious, non-conformity advanced in the lyrics listened to in my youth, didn't help matters. The majority of my life decisions have been made from this skewed perspective. Like cancer, I never felt comfortable as part of the whole. For years I aggressively worked for money, possessions, and prestige, but now, in defiance to societal values, I've discovered that these are the standards of a dying world and their hold on me is diminishing.

My change began when, through no conscious action of my own, I was placed in a situation over which I had very little control. I was forced to give up personal attachments to family, friends, possessions, career, and identity in a variety of life-altering situations. From this obligatory awakening I have concluded two very significant points: 1. that my idealistic plans rarely work, and 2. there is a Higher Power. Up to this point I had been afraid to leave situations in someone else's hands. I wasn't quite sure what they would do, and there was a level of mistrust and arrogance that no one could do things quite like me. I was uncomfortable with their understanding of my uniqueness. Maybe my files would be misplaced? Perhaps I would be viewed at a level below my perceived ability. Even worse, I might be so insignificant to not be seen as being useful at all.

Through this circumstance of facing my own emotional cancers, I learned about submission. I learned that to truly grow and overcome myself I needed to be willing to surrender my thoughts, my deeds, and my will to another. I learned that I needed to trust in a Higher Power and by so doing I became free to see beyond the immediacy of my situation. Then, and only then, was I able to more clearly acknowledge my own weakness and see my part in the downfall of my world. The cancer of my contempt for the natural order of things taught me to submit to others who know more than I do. By listening, by learning, and by surrendering my will, I am working to become healthy once again. I am healing and there are scars, but by submitting, I can overcome.

* * * * *

36. ACQUIESCENCE

Lately I've begun to realize that it's not what I do that is significant, but rather why I do it. My power to serve does not lie in resumes, references, or credentials. What I've done in the past or what I'm currently engaged in now is insignificant. My actual expression is often more important than the motive. Attitude is now more important than aptitude. This is a complete realignment of my reasoning. I now pray for the sense of purpose to be utilized as an instrument of peace, and with this I surrender my profession to a Higher Power.

Acquiescence in today's world is a rare behavior. It is a trait of quiet compliance that is currently unrewarded and socially shunned. Paramount in human dynamics is the struggle for power, supremacy, and dominance over the will of the other. From world politics to our athletic venues, the end result is a struggle for victory over oppression leading to overt self-sufficiency, self-reliance, and independence. Movies, gaming, and television programming all play out this same scenario: control through force and self-determination. Nice guys lose and the clever and the strong prevail. Sovereignty is valued above all. Freedom to choose for myself, to determine for me, and to manage my affairs regardless of the cost is the icon of the survivors in our world today.

Recently I had the opportunity to observe a young boy fight, as if for his very life, to retain self-governance. His youth was spent in the orphanages of Romania. What atrocities and mayhem he experienced in his early years we can only imagine. Obviously it was a cold, deliberate environment void of acceptance and love. Human touch was in the form of power and manipulation. His spirit rose up and rebelled. Now in the hands of a loving family, his inability to submit defied the very love he needed. Like a caged Bengal tiger, he paced, watched, and waited as memories of his past haunted his soul. But, why? Was his current environment unfit? Was he not loved? Was he unsafe, undernourished, and persecuted? Not in the least, but his past relentlessly plagued him. His inborn drive for self-rule was profound and it defied logic. Intently he rebelled against the love so freely offered in defense of his subconscious need to control what he could not.

This experience triggered a reflection upon my behavior, my motives, my responses, and my drives. Have I, like André, become so conditioned from the past that instinctively I refuse to submit? Acquiescence to spouse, to peers, to superiors, to any Higher Power is avoided in order to maintain control! My accomplishments to date are directly linked to my assertiveness and aggression. My pride lies in my ability to succeed on my own. But is this real? Is anyone truly self-made? In the grander context, I submit the answer to be, "NO!" Our very breath is a grace allotted in defined measure. As my thoughts continue, I begin to realize that to some degree all humanity struggles with this self-management issue. Arbitrary submission to the will of another is universally rejected. All of us struggle for the freedom to speak, to think, to choose, to elect, and to submit to another. To relent, to obey, or to willingly succumb, when unaware or anxious about the outcomes, defies natural man. It is predicated on a belief in a Higher Authority, and greater personal good. Without it we can never truly learn to follow. As with young André, this struggle rages until at some miraculous moment insecurities subside, walls diminish, our guard relaxes, and we sense our true motives towards the bigger picture. We don't comprehend all details. All we can hope for is an acknowledgment of the intent and the motives of a Higher Power whose only concern is our maximum joy; this is an understanding that we, here, today trapped in our worldly chains, cannot yet comprehend the glories that await.

* * * * *

37. CRITICAL KNOTS

A knot is a primitive method of securing a line in an attempt to protect a load. Designed to hold strong in times of stress when pressure is great, a slip results in unpredicted damage and catastrophic events unimagined at the time initiated. As a Boy Scout I learned many knots and mastered most. My objective was not a matter of holding cargo, but merely of mastery. Of them all, it was the square knot that became my greatest challenge. Performed in two efforts, the latter created my test: fold left or fold right?

Even today I'm not quite sure if it is left first or right first. It is a small action, but one with powerful results. Performed wrongly it can still hold adequately for light loads, and only when great masses are imposed does the importance of the exactness of the procedure reveal itself. Then and only then, when time is of the essence, does the significance of the final fold come to bear. It's during times of relative ease when the lines must be checked and the bindings secured, not in the midst of a ruinous circumstance. Timely maintenance of critical knots ensures safety during periods of stress where outcomes are critical.

* * * * *

38. RULES OF THE JUNGLE

The laws of nature, devoid of human interference and manipulation, can teach us many important lessons. In the jungle, for example, baby animals are naive, cute, cuddly, and adorable. Curious by nature, they understandably wander about unaware of the potential dangers which await them at every turn. Drawn to new experiences, the excitement and anticipation drives their exploration. The probability of young animals surviving to adulthood is extremely low in this setting. The mother is keenly aware of this; she remembers all too well the dangers of her past. So here we have the energetic new cub and the cautious mother, each with competing goals. Youth, totally unaware of the danger, combined with resistance to the doting parent, is a formula for failure. Maybe it is the first real bout with danger that awakens the cub to the reality that if she is to survive, she must learn, understand, and respect the rules of the jungle! Once mother and baby have a common understanding and objective, the possibility of survival and growth to maturity increases greatly.

Alongside these instincts for survival in the human realm lie natural desires, passions, lusts, and cravings. The wellspring of these emotions and behaviors appear in childhood, and lie dormant, waiting to be released at some unknown moment. Just like the curious lion cub of the jungle, we teach children to control these natural impulses through conscious, pre-determined will. Time and self-control, combined with mutual awareness is a beginning, but not even this combination ensures safety. Nonetheless, such primitive passions, refined desires, and accompanying skills must be controlled for survival of the species. The building of trusting relationships, based on a foundation of respect and loyalty, will enhance the level of survival in the jungle of life. Emotional and physical starvation is a sure way to sabotage existence. To be fit for survival in the jungle of life, the laws must be observed with strictness and with rigor.

* * * * *

39. THE RIGHT THING

All my life, I have endeavored to do "the right thing," as if there was an absolute black and white, good and bad, and right or wrong approach. As I've matured I begin to realize that in many cases there is no right decision. It is more the process and intent of the decision that is paramount. What about the right action for the wrong reason? If any good is accomplished, is it lost in the motive? Often I find myself reluctantly engaged in good causes when somewhere between then and now I get the true meaning and my heart changes. The opposite can also be true. Engaged in inappropriate actions, impressions reveal the behavior in its whole context and I modify my course accordingly.

The most challenging situation for me is working with the complex dynamic of multiple players where what is right for one does not hold true for the others. Does global rightness outweigh personal relevance? Or does that perspective alone eliminate, or at least hamper, personal choice? Organizations, regardless of their size or impact, have established boundaries and rules that protect and promote the betterment of the whole. In most cases this protects the rights of the individuals, but occasionally exceptions occur. Then there is the case where jointly all parties are in agreement and they make the right decisions, but the outcome is not as expected. In fact, simultaneous digression reduces the conditions to a point where a defiant action would have been less damaging.

Can we mutually agree that a life beyond this mere existence is anticipated? If that is possible, does rightness transcend the grave? Are temporal judgments and perspectives finite, and thereby linked to the two-dimensional realm of understanding? In such a case the only sound viewpoint becomes one of context more than event. Timeless variables beyond our current scope may in fact be operating in a greater scheme of order, time, and measure.

As such, my context of rightness becomes critical in order to avoid compromising the grander design. This broader perspective frees me to back off a bit, become more accepting of happenings, and more tolerant of self and others. We cannot change the course of time. We can only, in sincere desire, make choices which become labeled as positive or negative over time. Given sufficient time, even my current failures begin to take on eternal meaning and significance.

Is nobility and greatness determined more by the strength of the fight and the valiancy of the defeated than the mere outcome of the battle? Is honor reserved for those who retain integrity regardless of the result? Is the right thing always right?

* * * * *

40. DON'T SHOP HUNGRY

On the rare occasion that I formally go grocery shopping, I have witnessed radical departures from the logical and practical when deprived of food for an extended period of time. Everything begins to look good, even brussel sprouts! In this weakened state, it is amazing what becomes a necessity. Price and value are instantly minor considerations when compared to filling my famished form. The primeval drive for food overpowers logic and reason. Under the philosophy of something now as opposed to more and better tomorrow, many of us devour the present with no thought of the future. Research indicates that those who can delay gratification generally grow up better adjusted, more confident, and extremely dependable. Those who succumb to the immediate gratification of self, tend to be challenge avoidant, easily frustrated, seriously stubborn, and more prone to buckle under stress. The ability to wait, even when it is inconvenient and difficult, leads to freedom, power, and financial independence.

Impulse buying is the mainstay of retail. Grocery stores locate essentials near the rear of the facility forcing consumers to pass aisle after aisle of non-essential impulse purchases both coming and going. Fifty percent of the sales volume is determined by this phenomenon. Money truly has wings. The world is designed to take our wealth, and we have learned well to consume and spend. Addictive over-consumption is witnessed by the size of our homes and the thickness of our waists. So, when shopping, don't go hungry, but instead go with focused purpose.

* * * * *

41. FROM GETTING TO GIVING

During the D-Day Invasion of World War II only a handful of Generals oversaw the entire campaign from Central Headquarters. Few if any of the front line Commanders were aware of the entire scope of the plan and most knew only enough to perform their assigned duty. Their movements and objectives were monitored closely, and adjustments were initiated as needed to accommodate for the performance of others. They willingly placed their lives, and the lives of those in their command, in harm's way without the luxury of even knowing why. These leaders on the front were not chosen for their creativity or intelligence, but solely on their ability to put self interest aside and follow instructions with exactness. They expressed complete trust in the general intelligence behind the orders, and strict obedience to the command. This is what led to that great victory which turned the tide of the entire war.

All my life I have idealized the independent thinker and the creative soul. I went about selling my ideas to achieve my objectives. Even when the outcome was often in support to another, I was still on my own, the lone wolf selling in the hopes of getting. Today my perspective has altered. Today my outlook has changed. Today my vantage point has moved. Getting has shifted to giving, and selling to serving. Getting involves selling. It implies that I don't have enough and that I need more. I must sell this viewpoint to be happy. Giving, on the other hand, is a statement of abundance, and that I can afford to share. Service is the offering of support to those in need. Giving service puts me in a position to look out for others. They, not I, are the object of my attention. Those military leaders on the battle lines years ago knew this simple truth. They knew that you really only get to keep those things that you give away. Years later, many grateful nations still honor their offerings.

* * * * *

42. WHAT TO DO

We spend the majority of our waking hours, in fact the bulk of our lives, engaged in our professions and careers. It seems that the more lucrative the job, the greater the attendant time demands and pressures. Stressful work environments create stressed out people, stressed out relationships, and stressed out families. It's very difficult to turn off the job just because you walk in the front door. The adrenaline keeps pumping long after the environment has changed. Work place stress becomes home life stress. Spouses, children, and events are dealt with just like troublesome clients and staff. Even minor delays and disappointments at home are overreacted to, given this heightened sensitivity. Many of us live by the motto that time is money, and things rarely seem to flow smoothly enough! Few jobs out there are immune from these demands. Even the "slower paced" occupations have been required to "step up" in order to compete.

I've spent the past 25 years of my adult life reviewing organizations, assisting management in determining goals, assessing current conditions, and then facilitating the transition. I've done this long enough that it has become second nature. As I enter situations, facilities, or relationships I quickly determine the maximum improvement for the minimal cost or effort; "low hanging fruit" I call it. I've recently discovered that without a sincere, conscious, sustained effort to stop this process of thinking, I'm halfway into it before I realize there is no contract and no one has asked for my assessment!

Because of the dynamic, diverse world in which we live, we as individuals are changing, adapting, and evolving. I have heard that every seven years our personality is measurably different. This in a large part must be due to the impact of our professions. To modify this trend we must become keenly aware of our individual situations, and willfully develop methods of leaving work outside of our homes. It begins with understanding, but it doesn't stop there. Without conscious, deliberate, and sustained effort our families can become victims to our overly-committed, excessively-stressed lifestyles. Relationships become causalities, assets are lost, and families declare emotional bankruptcy. "What" I do must be limited to "where" I can best do it without negatively impacting my home life.

43. SOFT AND MUSHY

When a generation of youth exists in a state of abundance and ease, it creates a soft and mushy mentality. I think it comes from lack of genuine personal challenges. We are all born self-centered and as such, we rarely elect to impose challenges upon ourselves just for the practice. There is a prevailing belief that in order for life to be good, we have to avoid pain and discomfort. We become so accomplished at pain avoidance that we begin to feel nothing. We feel no pain, no joy, and no hope. Even love becomes increasingly difficult to identify.

The current state of much of the developed world is that of abundance. The immediate world exists to gratify me personally. Things are so good physically that it's hard to see beyond the moment. As a result, we tend to set our objective on personal security and comfort, which is truly a moving target. The more we achieve, the greater our needs, and we never seem able to fully meet these ever-growing wants.

Service to others appears to be the pivotal change agent. If we can genuinely attain a point where joy is experienced in the service of others, this attitude can change us from soft and mushy to firm and hard-working. Often we engage in duty bound service and sharing, and if we persist, the sensation of joy can be experienced. It requires faith to make the leap from self to others. The strength of any union is bound on this principle that the good of the whole is good for me as well. Service to others, even the unlikable, strengthens the whole.

By design we naturally evolve and mature through the passages of life, being forced to situations of increasing responsibility. Parallel to this is the opportunity to place others first. If self-pleasure, personal satisfaction, ease, and immediate gratification dominate our focus, the change from soft and mushy will never transpire. Placing others first elicits independence and joy, but it begins with short term sacrifices, difficulties, and pain. Choosing inconvenience and pain over pleasure and enjoyment is a worthy lesson. Trials force us to internalize our convictions. No one sets out to be nothing. No one wants to be unmotivated, lifeless, and lazy. No one desires to be soft and mushy.

44. TITLES AND LABELS

Doctor, President, Chancellor. Titles such as these are assigned by organizations to recognize accomplishments, identify accountability, classify responsibility, and distinguish capability. It is a time proven method of acknowledgment for a life of industry, effort, and effectiveness.

Failure, Loser, Useless. These labels are assigned to people to describe lives of sloth, misdirection, and laziness. Are such labels accurate, correct, justified, or deserving? Often misfortune, misunderstanding, or insecurity are the true causes for lack of industry. These labels don't motivate, encourage, or support. They merely limit growth, prevent change, and hamper development.

Beyond safety and survival, we humans strive for notoriety and distinction. Great sacrifices of time, money, and effort are invested in the hopes of attaining the desired title or label. Missing the mark often results in assignment of the latter. But why? As supportive and helpful as the titles are at encouraging greatness, the labels can be equally damaging and destructive.

Plans are made, priorities are chosen, and energy is expelled in the struggle to achieve. Even with the most elaborate campaigns, unforeseen obstacles thwart our objectives. Unanticipated events disrupt or even divert our very progression. Achievement of my objective is only attainable through dedication, determination, and endurance. But all is not equal: roads vary, paths are unique, and sojourns become exclusive. The non-realization of goals does not convey the effort and abilities sacrificed, just as awards don't always validate worthiness. We are all different. Mine is a unique journey tailored through destiny and choice. No one sets out to fail. No one strives to lose. Each of us confronts a series of unique events to maximize personal growth. In failure, as in success, a man's dignity is revealed. We are free to choose how unanticipated and unplanned events affect us. Past mistakes may either improve us or neutralize us. It is our choice.

Titles and labels are powerful external variables. Negative labels never help. At best, they provide momentary satisfaction to the giver, but always discouragement to the labeled, which only serves to compound the present challenges.

To strive and fail is far superior than to have never tried at all. So many of us are numbed by the fear of failure. We are neutralized by risk, and stagnated by threat. This journey does not end with death. Our path proceeds beyond the limitations of life. The final tally is not taken now, nor is it set by popular opinion. Present failures lead to future accomplishments that are often unattainable without current setbacks. It's not what happens to us that is significant, but rather how we respond to what happens. Obstacles taken on, challenges risen above, and setbacks confronted all build character that can be developed in no other way. This earned temperament and integrity, superior to earthly riches, rises with us in our journey.

Ours is the option to choose. Do I choose discouragement or optimism? Do I learn from the past or does the past dictate my future? Do I admit mistakes or does pride ensnare me? Do I work for titles or accept labels? The short term perspective of the ego cannot be allowed to dominate our choices! The fear of failure must not neutralize us!

* * * * *

45. THE CLOCK KEEPS TICKING

All of us know that we are going to die some day. Possibly this knowledge alone is why we hold onto the precious moments of life. In spite of this awareness, we spend a lot of time on necessary but somewhat frivolous things: we drive cars, we wash cloths, we go to the dentist, and we buy shoes. We use precious hours each day sleeping, eating, cleaning, and buying gifts sometimes for people we don't even know or care for. As such, it is easy to see why we must be choosy in how we spend our leisure time. It is understandable that we are often self absorbed and stingy with our limited resource of time.

I believe that time is our greatest personal asset. It is time that we invest for the generation of money, which in turn can be used to provide greater leisure time. How do we get beyond this ritualistic routine existence, executed relentlessly through generations of habitual reinforcement? There must be a better way to manage our time, a greater use for our time, and a wiser investment of our time.

To achieve control over this greatest asset requires a high order of commitment, and a keen sense of prioritizing tasks and obligations. This disciplined thinking enables us to consecrate our time to its best possible use. To consecrate something means to dedicate or devote it to a chosen purpose. When we choose to make the best possible use of our time, we must submit our emotions, thoughts, and behavior to this chosen purpose. This is not easy. Past ways of thinking and doing must disappear, or the transition will not happen and the end results will be disastrous. Engaging in partial service at a level of minimums won't suffice either. We take great pride in our accomplishments, our possessions, and our offerings, but a consecration of time requires more than the token acts of humanity offered as a matter of convenience.

We, of like heart and mind, must cling together. Not from a perspective of personal need but for the promise of mutual synergistic potential. The crutches of the past including relationships, positions, titles, and things must take on a submissive status. When we decide to move to the next level it requires determination and commitment, which in turn will sustain us during the low periods. Just as the young child who becomes completely fascinated with a simple ball cannot begin to comprehend the workings of a car let alone the physics of flight, so are we similarly limited. Even with these limitations, it does not prohibit the child from riding in the car to the airport and flying to a distant location.

* * * * *

46. BALANCE OF POWER

The ancient Hopi occupied the Southwestern States nearly one thousand years ago. Did they vanish as history suggests, or are they living with us now? If not physically, they at least may remain in spirit. Often a glance at yesterday can enlighten us today. Frequently, past perspectives can refocus the present. Seldom are earnest self-reflections destructive. In review, the core belief which bound the Hopi together then, can provide strength to our present condition.

To the Hopi civilization, the family, the dwelling house, and the field were inseparable. The woman was the heart of these, and the ownership rested with her. The man cultivated the field, but he rendered its harvest into the woman's keeping. The man built the house, but the woman was its owner because she repaired and preserved it. The man planted the seed, but the woman grew it, delivered it, and nurtured it, creating and sustaining the family.

Today the world provides women little convincing direction for the process of achieving long-lasting happiness in womanhood. There are conflicting worldly advisers on every side, seeming to agree only that old ways are to be rejected and replaced by roles that discount these ancient truths. Are women to be men? Must they compete to be equal? Are not men and women unique in so many ways? A woman's willful rejection of her uniqueness not only affects her, but influences generations that follow. Each woman chooses whether to accept her divine responsibilities or to embrace the counterfeits. Is there peril in following the world's destructive advice?

The balance of power in the Hopi world was initiated by the man but sustained by the woman. Rather than equal in position and calling, they were unique and separate, yet symbiotically dependent upon each other. There was a balance of power because they were equal in objective and purpose, but radically different in function.

* * * * *

47. CONFIRMATION

At half way to age 100 I've taken some time lately to assess my life's activities and general purpose. Under review, I wonder if my past accomplishments are as well off as my future goals? My efficiency is contrasted against my effectiveness at the tasks I've chosen to invest my most valuable resource in, that of my time. As mortality becomes a reality, personal priorities change. How do we know when our energies have been well directed, that our offerings have been accepted? Is it similar to business where we are measured by our bottom-line? Is the accumulation of hard assets the measure of stability? Does market dominance ensure future success? Does the end justify the means? As CEO do I have a fiduciary responsibility to show strong quarterly profits regardless of the long-term consequences?

Our lives are a testament to our motives. Knowing that I am engaged in the right activity, at the right time, with the right people is an indescribable sensation. It is now becoming my life's objective, measurable by a confirmation of rightness, of truth, and of peace. As a by-product of actions and attitudes, I strive for a greater sense of belonging and acceptance. Is my life on-track with a grander plan? A confirmation of this personal purpose is validation that efforts are appropriate and accepted. This spirit of confirmation comes in the form of peace, and it is available to all who seek it. Using personal choice to direct my life's efforts in pursuit of higher purpose is the meaning of life. My assets have now become my history!

* * * * *

48. DISCONTENT

Why do we strive for that which is beyond our grasp? Why do we pretend we are more than our current measure? Never content in the process of becoming, our discontent overcomes us. We become possessed with wanting, needing, and finally craving. Spiraling out of control, we are never able to accomplish enough, never able to obtain enough, and never able to be enough. Never being enough breeds further discontent. Our latest accomplishment is merely the failure for tomorrow's success. Goals, improvement, and refinement are all part of our plan, but we can never quite arrive. How often is the object of our desire only an illusion, a fantasy, or a mirage? I need this! I want this? I can't live without that! Every one has one but me!

I recently spent some serious time on the Southern California coast doing architectural work. Laguna, Huntington, Redondo: these beaches are all pretty much the same. I've been there as a tourist, but never as a native. No doubt about it, I love the beach! The Pacific Ocean with its white sand and the palms swaying in the gentle ocean breeze is addicting. Soon my mind begins fantasying about living here. Paradise! These places cost five times that of a similar place elsewhere in the city, but think of all that sand! And what about the money I'd stow away by not going on vacations, or to movies, or amusement parks. The gas savings alone is significant, let alone the environmental statement it would make riding a bike everywhere. Five hours into the project and I'm sold on the idea. Rent a place at first, with an option to buy when my income catches up to my needs. In another life I owned a home on acres of land seven times larger than this one, at one-third the price, but think of the money I'd be making in appreciation. It's an investment. I have now had this new self-image of retired beach surfer-type for about an hour and a half, and I'm starting to really identify with it! It will be hard now to visualize myself anywhere but here: the beautiful people, the excitement, the ocean, the beach. Yes, we can't forget about the beach.

I'm awakened from my fantasy by the opening of the door. Ron, the project manager, arrives and we begin to talk. As it turns out he was also caught up by the "rapture of the beach." First he bought a condo, then a small home, and finally a large one. "Initially we went to the beach three times a day," Ron gloated. "You couldn't keep us away." Then, as his need for a bigger residence grew and the demands on his time increased, he set himself a goal of going to the beach once a week, but, he reluctantly admitted, he rarely made it. Now that he has a palatial estate in walking distance from the beach, he hasn't made it to the inviting white sands in over three months. He now sells beachfront real estate on the beach that he never visits. Too busy! Too tired! Too much effort!

Why are we never content? Why must we always want more? Why do we not appreciate how truly fortunate we are to have what we have? A rich person is one who makes more than she spends and has more than she wants. It's not where you live but how you live. We exist in a world of abundance yet we all believe we need more. Only as I align this understanding with my actions can I achieve contentment.

* * * * *

49. WHEN I GET A BREAK

In a past life I was a busy soul. I was always engaged in some activity of supreme importance that I believed was pivotal to everyone's well being. So much of my life took a back row seat to these critical tasks. Relationships, one-time events, and small irreplaceable moments of history were lost to seemingly bigger and more important things because the job had to get done regardless of the cost. People's lives were on the line. "Anyway," I consoled myself, "when there is a break I will mend the fences."

Life has a way of moving forward in hyper speed, and the small "breaks" come and go without much notice. Patterns of choice don't change much; the "breaks" fill in with other essential matters of importance. Then, if we are lucky, something unbelievable happens, like a 7.4 earthquake in Northridge, California, which turns life upside down. Sadly, there are some casualties, but it's the collateral damage that is life changing because it represents a total breakdown of the infrastructure. Even the most basic services shut down. So much of my confidence in my fast-paced, important life was based upon the illusion that this delicate balance would never fall.

Well, life changed for me, and now I have all the time in the world. My "breaks" are endless. The worst thing that you can do to a workaholic is to provide him with no work. Instantly my heart turned to loved ones, the rejected masses of my past. Why won't they call me? Don't they care? It's been 17 ½ hours, don't they know that I'm going crazy here! Once initial concerns are positively confirmed about health and wellness, they all go back about their own busy lives. Too much like their father, I guess. These accomplished men and women are now changing the world in their own way. They are important, pivotal members of a complex society. When they have a "break" they will call, they will mend fences then.

My life changed in an instant. I got the connection. I still have time to make a difference.

* * * * *

50. MAMA

I was talking to a young man the other day who has become a dear friend over the last few years. Our thoughts migrated to talk of marriage and responsibility. I asked if he was married or had a steady girlfriend. He stated that he had a girlfriend, but that he wasn't ready to marry her. Although the desire to have kids was exciting, it was currently out of his financial grasp. This discussion led to the following story.

I was in the 6th grade and after a particularly boring day at school I came home and announced to Mama that I didn't want to go to school any more. "Okay," she said, "but you will have to get a job and help out with the bills." My dad had left years before. The next morning I went out and began asking neighbors if I could mow their lawns. Most agreed and I was in heaven: lots of money, freedom, and no school bells. After a couple of weeks I had covered the neighborhood and was in need of a new way to earn money. After some deep thought, I decided to go to the local swap meet and see if anyone there could use some help putting-up or taking-down their booths. Before long I was helping everyone from sun-up to sun-down. Soon I had accumulated $150 cash, which was a lot for a 13 year old boy living in Redondo, California back then.

I was feeling pretty good about myself so one morning I said, "Mama, I need to go to the mall to buy some cool shoes." She said, "No, you don't have enough money." I protested loudly and proudly showed her my newly earned cash. Turning away, she proceeded to write down a list of all the bills required to keep me safe, warm, and full: rent, utilities, food, clothing, medicine. I was amazed at how much it cost. She then took half of my hard earned money and put it in her purse, and I walked away feeling I had gotten a bargain.

A few months later I decided that I needed to return to school. I also found a permanent job for minimum wage at a local tire store. I couldn't wait to tell Mama the good news. Exhausted after running the entire way home, I arrived and blurted out my good news. Calmly she said that I could now pay the Cable TV bill. A few months later, I received a raise and upon telling Mama was informed that I could now pay the water bill. After a while I caught on and quit informing Mama of my financial successes.

By the time I was nearing 16, I had saved over $800 and so I began looking for cars. I found a 1968 Chevelle SS for only $700. I couldn't believe my luck; I would have the greatest car at school. I ran home to Mama asking her if I could buy it. She said that we could go look at it tomorrow. When we arrived she didn't say much, so I concluded that it was a deal and we were good to go. The next day was Saturday and my excitement made it difficult to work. At quitting time I ran home as fast as I could. Bursting in the front door I asked Mama when we could go and buy the car. She looked directly at me and said that there were six reasons why I wasn't going to get the car: Math, English, History, Biology, PE and Science. Of all the disappointments of my life, this was the greatest I had experienced to date. Over the next week I went by daily to look at my car. It took days before I was willing to accept reality. All that was left to do was study, for I knew that Mama wasn't budging. Within the next quarter my grades began to improve. Within another six months they were quite respectable. Unfortunately by now the car was gone. It was then that I realized that I had in fact survived without the '68 Chevelle that I had desired so intently.

As my young friend's story came to a close, he stated, "So here I am today. I own my truck, I have a nice apartment, and plenty of food. I wish I would have gone to college but I got comfortable with my life and time just got away from me. As I think about the costs of buying a home, raising kids, and still enjoying life I don't think it is time yet. I'm not sexually active because I don't want to risk having a kid I can't afford." On that note my service was complete, and so we shook hands and said good bye.

Well Jose, I have thought about our conversation quite a lot over the last few days. Even though you have regrets for not taking advantage of additional schooling, I believe you learned a lesson far superior, and one that is in great need by the youth of today. You learned to delay gratification in an age of self absorption. You learned how to accept responsibility for your actions in an age of entitlement. You learned how to apply yourself and work hard to achieve in an age of laziness. You learned how to control your emotions in an age of egocentric outbursts. You learned that firmness and denial builds character if offered in love. Yes, Jose, you possess attributes rare in today's world. And yes, Jose, when you do arrive at that point in life that you feel ready to accept the obligations of a wife and family you will be a wonderful husband and father. You will be a father strong enough to pass on those wonderful values taught to you by your Mama.

* * * * *

51. ANGELS AND ME

Current public opinion reveals a strong belief in angels, stronger now than in years past. Books, music, television and talk shows all echo the sentiment of the possibility of angels. Are we merely seeking comfort, peace, and belonging, and angels provide that end, or are they real, tangible and available to all who truly need help?

Originally a God-fearing people, many nations have slowly slumped away from the dogmatic traditions of the past. Yet, in spite of our callousness, the question remains, "Why are we here?" Do angels help bridge the gap between a Higher Power and humanity? Beyond specific creeds and out of religious context, do angels surface and are they available to aid anyone? Are they servants commissioned to deliver divine messages and assist the needy? Do they arrive in human form? Are they wise, powerful and liberated from death? Do they have wings, white robes, and halos? The key is not their form, but the message they deliver.

The divinely recorded angelic messages of the past impacted the world. Now, it seems, angelic appearances are taking on the common, the practical, and the ordinary. Like danger avoidance, pain assistance, and time sensitive interventions, their visits are important, but not earth shattering. Maybe this is why we question their existence: a stranger who stops to carry a heavy load for me, an unexpected call from a neighbor, a dream which provides needed comfort in a time of sorrow, an unlikely hand when assistance was required. Do angels straddle the line between two separate worlds, or are they just random occurrences out of context? Does validating of the notion of angels follow the larger issue of confirming a Higher Power?

However you look at it, angels point to the existence of a Higher Power. To those whose lives have been affected by them, they are more than chance events. Angels are not a replacement for a Higher Power but are an additional source of comfort and support. They are manifest as divine entities from another world, or as neighbors providing timely service. They ease my burden, they minimize my pain, and they encourage me to believe the best of people. Once affected, my charge is to do likewise: to return the blessing wherever, whenever, however, and to whomever

I can. Perhaps this is the divine message that does impact the world. Perhaps this message is grander than the past. Perhaps these random angelic acts of kindness promote contagious assistance to others. What a thought: divine answers to prayer through me. Even I can be an angel!

* * * * *

52. ROLLER COASTERS AND CAROUSELS

A roller coaster theory of life suggests that we excitedly buy a ticket and then willingly let ourselves be strapped into a seat. The ride starts out slow, like the little train being pulled to the top of the first peak. From this point, gravity takes over, and all you can do is hang on for dear life. It is exhilarating. It is nerve wracking. It is over in a brief moment. Many call it insane, illogical, and silly. In contrast to the roller coaster, many choose the carousel. It is predictable, controlled, safe, and conventional. Some might even say it is mundane. One lifestyle is not better than the other, they are just different, and one can learn important lessons from both styles. The trick I think is to maintain sincerity regardless of the path chosen.

I have always loved roller coasters, and my life choices have maintained this thrill-seeking lifestyle. As a result I have walked many paths alone. Real adventurers, I fear, are becoming an artifact of the past. But if you have ever risked beyond your level of comfort, you will understand that there is no exhilaration like that which overtakes us by accident. I have no regrets for living an adventurous, roller coaster life. What I have learned from my daring exploits is that there are far more roads on which you may traverse life's paths than those that seem to have been predetermined for you by others. Become a song, and ride the winds and tides. Follow the melody of the ocean leading to your appointed shore. Let your final notes reverberate in the air as they ring true to the life you lived.

* * * * *

53. DESTRUCTIVE REINFORCEMENT

A long time ago I recall learning much about behaviorism and classical conditioning. You may remember the old stimulus response stuff from high school psychology. Years later during college, tutors took the theory even farther introducing me to the concept of what they labeled Destructive Reinforcement. This term describes the phenomenon of unintentionally rewarding undesirable behavior. Take the typical 6th grade class that is beginning to act up. The teacher threatens additional math homework unless they regain focus. Now we all know that math proficiency in American schools is lacking. A lot of the problems can be attributed to general student attitude and subsequent practice and study. By using math homework as the punishment for misbehavior, the teacher is declaring that math is bad, math is negative, and math is punishment. Contrast this to the words uttered daily in Japan or China that math is good, math is powerful, and math is essential. This is destructive reinforcement.

How often are we guilty of this in our daily interactions? Our words sound right, reasonable, and good but our actions speak louder, unintentionally reinforcing undesired behavior. My words may say, "I accept you," "I love you," "I'll protect you," but my actions shout, "I am intolerant," "I am insincere," and "I am insecure." Political correctness often leads us into these circumstances. We speak the words that are expected and acceptable, but we behave in a contrary manner. We perpetuate destructive reinforcement. Your actions speak so loudly I can't hear your words.

* * * * *

54. WITHOUT CONDITION

I have been involved in a lot of negotiations in my life. An extensive list of conditions is always included with any deal. A transaction is a contract documenting the exchange of goods and services. Both parties must spell out individual performance requirements to determine overall contentment. If one party falls short in completing their part of the bargain, actions are initiated against that individual in an attempt to force compliance. Corrective actions are penalizing in nature. The value of the agreement is determined by the degree of compliance to the pre-arranged contract.

In contrast, unconditional arrangements transcend the individual behavior of those involved. Like the gentleman's handshake of long ago, its strength, its bound, and its power was based upon the integrity of the individuals involved. In an unconditional arrangement, negative pressure is rarely brought against the noncompliant individual and this maintains the pureness, the strength, and the integrity of the relationship. This type of pact is established for mutual benefit, regardless of the level of compliance by either party. This freedom allows both parties to openly and willingly choose to honor the agreement at whatever level they choose.

Any relationship is a contract. It is conditional in the sense that both parties agree to love and serve in exchange for love and service. It is unconditional when reciprocal love is exchanged freely without restrictions. Typically in a relationship, when the love is not transferred equally, sanctions and punitive conditions emerge naturally. As conditions are placed on a relationship, performance and evaluation requirements emerge, and the unconditional accepting nature of the arrangement changes also. Children placed in this environment will reflect the same attitude as demonstrated between the adults. That's the power of it.

Everyone desires the feeling of pure, unqualified acceptance. Behavior, positive or negative, can be accepted or rejected, but individual worth, approval, and belonging continues without conditions. Unconditional love can never be employed in excess, nor can you err in redundancy. The message must ring clear from your heart and words in spite of actions and behaviors. You are loved for who you are. You are admitted, accepted, and appreciated as you are. You are cherished, treasured and esteemed unconditionally! I accept you with all our baggage. I accept you with open arms, not under conditions or sanctions, but as you are. I love you without condition.

* * * * *

55. INTENT

Who ever knows the true intent of the heart? Who can discern the true meaning of another's thoughts? Who can determine how plans were made, events initiated, or outcomes documented? What about actions? Can anyone ever know the motivator? Others looking in, at best, have a clouded view based upon partial data. At worst, a whole myriad of emotions drive the conclusion. Even from a personal perspective, my view is distorted. Even conscious claims of high personal integrity are biased.

Could it be that long ago in a galaxy far, far away, we were all full of integrity, all sincere, all true, and all genuine? Could it be that time, experience, and failure have created the superficial world we now occupy? Given the barrage of insincerity in relationships, is it any wonder that valid actions are alleged as false, that sincere gestures are perceived as counterfeit, and that legitimate offerings are rejected as manipulations? How in this world of cynicism can the genuine prevail, or the true flourish? Is integrity a dying belief?

As I personally question my own integrity, I wonder if my motives for past actions are as I once believed? What was the true source and ultimate driver? After a series of shortsighted judgments and unfortunate circumstances, I could become callused, cynical, and defensive. The hurt of cankering gossip waged thoughtlessly against me or in turn against others can dehumanize me if I let it. In self-preservation I vow to never again offer, never again assist, and never again risk. But wait! I don't want to live like that. I am unwilling to react in kind to this distrustful world where I exist. As such, I regroup, I reevaluate, I recommit, and I grow. I know that only I will determine my actions. I know that only I will determine my responses. I know that only I will evaluate the intent of my motives. If wrongly judged, I will let it pass. If falsely accused, I will seek to ignore. If inaccurately evaluated, I will rise above. In this way I will honor my personal integrity through consistent thought and action.

* * * * *

56. DECEPTION

What are the facts? What is the truth? Who started it? Who's wrong? Who's right? Our lives are a seamless stream of events and situations which demand honesty and rightness. Some such circumstances have a major impact in our lives, others are minor, and many go unnoticed. At such times, it is often difficult to maintain integrity because egos scream, "Say what you need to say to protect yourself, to defend yourself, and to advance yourself!"

Accidents and mishaps are natural byproducts of life. It is easy to become callused by over-reacting to every physical or emotional bump or bruise. It is easy to wonder if they are accidental or committed with intention? Who will ever know? Are they conscious acts of aggression or mere by-products of our fast-paced society? When an incident of significance occurs, self-preservation thrusts us into our defense mode almost without thought. This primitive drive to survive is as old as man. Without reason, our perspectives have evolved to a point that it's hard to conceive that one event drove both. The pendulum swings, accelerating with each added push. Individuals begin justifying actions and behavior. It is at these times when blame and accusations arise that we are faced with the dilemma of integrity. Will my words and actions be consistent with what I know is true and right?

As details of a particular incident or mishap are repeatedly retold to sympathetic, curious listeners, the facts easily grow legs and the differing perspectives are now moving, sliding, crawling, and running further apart. Polarization occurs through self-preservation. Truth and reality have now become personal. The initial event is now just a shadow of the actual occurrence. Defensiveness has led to justification. Battle lines are drawn, allies are recruited, and the combat has begun. But, what really happened? Was it intentional or a mere accident? What was the intent? Were the motives innocent or with malice? What is real? Loved ones become alienated and have forgotten, or are not ready to take responsibility for their actions. Everyone wants the truth but few strive for reason! Rational thought and understanding are now vanishing commodities. Sadly, all are deceived. This process has no innocent victims, nor even innocent participants. The deception of partial truths devalues personal integrity and all share in the loss.

57. THE TRAILER

I had a friend borrow my flatbed trailer a while back. Upon return I discovered that it was littered with trash, wood, and debris. The next time it was used, a stop to the dump was required before I was able to proceed. Maybe he was in a hurry and knew that I wouldn't mind helping him out? Maybe he forgot? Maybe he felt his time was more valuable than mine? Not a big deal I guess, but inconvenient still the same. Weeks later an acquaintance called and asked if a friend of his, whom I didn't know, could borrow the trailer. I reluctantly agreed and the trailer was gone. After a few days I became concerned that it had not been returned. I had never met the borrower and for all I knew he had damaged it or worse. I decided that I would give him another couple of days before I got aggressive. Yes, a few more days of grace, but if it wasn't returned then he would face my wrath. Two days later I called my friend and inquired about the trailer. He explained to me that the person who had used it had, upon completion, decided to repaint it. Halfway through the project his daughter was hurt in an accident, which set the whole project on hold.

This was a great trailer, heavy duty with a winch and ramps. It was ideal for hauling cars, trash, furniture, or just general stuff. I had owned it for five years and in that time it had started to show its age. I always maintained it mechanically, but the appearance had been neglected. When the trailer was finally returned a few weeks later, it looked new again. I was speechless. Fortunately I had held my tongue. Fortunately I had resisted over-reacting.

A few days later I had a moment to reflect on the two events. In comparison, the first borrower's attitude was one of disrespect. It screamed, "My time is more valuable than yours." The latter borrower's behavior was obviously one of gratitude expressed in sacrifice and service. Although a small thing, a great truth was told about both people. It's interesting to note that the first had amassed great wealth and possessions, while the latter struggles at an hourly wage to meet monthly obligations. My point is not to judge the first, but rather to recognize and admire the latter. Here is someone who validates his personal integrity through his actions. Here is someone who is worthy of my respect. Here is someone whose behavior should be emulated. These are the type of people who truly make a difference in the world.

* * * * *

58. FIDUCIARY RESPONSIBILITY

Awhile back I made the mistake of entering into a business arrangement with a long-time family friend. I know in hindsight this was a grave mistake, but at the time it made sense. The strange thing about money and relationships is that they just never mix. From the start things did not go well, and over time they got progressively worse. Hoping for a turn in events, we continued to log time and materials into a deteriorating situation. Eventually we arrived at a point of impasse. Emotions were high and funds had stopped. Our friendship had been taxed to the max, but I still felt it would prevail due to the duration, depth, and breadth of it. Negotiations stalemated and litigation seemed imminent. Being sensitive to the situation, my friend and his wife came by our home one Sunday evening. Small talk aside, we began discussing our history together, the project and ultimately his company's position.

The entire problem could have been resolved by an easy concession. My entire life was but an ink spot on his bottom line, but that wasn't the issue here. The concern was about precedence? What if "the company" developed a reputation of concession? What if "the company" lost its standing of dominance, supremacy, and conquest? Others would come, and eventually moral issues would give way to nuisance cases. This would not be in "the company's" best interest now, would it? So a line had to be drawn here and now. Then came the words that still ring in my ears: "fiduciary responsibility." He stated directly, confidently, and affirmatively that because of his position with "the company," he had no choice. His fiduciary responsibility to his board and investors removed all options. Like a "Get Out of Jail Quick" card, he was off the hook. The dilemma was now resolved, for him at least.

Then, as if his declaration of fiduciary responsibility wasn't enough, he then went on to convey his confidence in the position established. He stated that the technology I had invented most likely existed in "the company's" files somewhere. He talked of the ease of backdating drawings. Additionally, he felt obliged to enlighten me to the realities of litigation against "the company." A small business can never keep up with the hundreds of thousands of dollars thrown at situations like this. With pockets that deep, time alone would surely kill my small company as they strung out the legal game. Regardless of the morality, the money ruled. He seemed relieved now, as if he had done me a great favor.

Under the guise of fiduciary responsibility, he was, in fact, under legal obligation to perform his corporate duty in support of "the company's" best interest. Fiduciary responsibility is a term created to provide executives an officially authorized directive to transcend honesty. Does this mean that if it is legal it must then be moral? If it is defensible in court then executives must perform to it? Fiduciary responsibility is the ability to transcend ethics, integrity, and truth. How convenient that he could maximize "the company's" interest at the sake of an irrelevant entity such as my fledgling company. Wasn't it convenient that because of his fiduciary responsibility he could do all this with little or no residual guilt? It wasn't about money as this man made over two million dollars annually for many years. This act, insignificant to him, set in motion the dismantling of many lives.

What is wrong with American business? When did a handshake lose its importance? When did a man's word lose its significance? When did corporate greed and short term returns bypass truthfulness and decency? My company was not an Enron, Worldcom, Tyco or even Arthur Andersen, but just a small company in a small city. Our passing was inconsequential and without notice to the world at large. We became just another casualty amongst the myriad of similar victims of war in the business world. Like so many others, we became the fatalities of decaying business ethics, crumbling business values, and decomposing business standards resulting in a general slumping towards obsessive greed and depravity.

* * * * *

59. RANGE ROVER

Up front, before you read further, let me present this disclaimer: My intent in this reflection is to make you uncomfortable, uneasy, and feeling a little guilty. I do this not to the point of discouragement, but as a wake up call sufficient to lead to change. The weak in character should read no further.

Today I pulled into a parking lot beside two brand new Range Rover HSE Sport vehicles. Yes, of course they were supercharged; how else could they generate the 510-horse power necessary to traverse the foreboding landscape between home and the office? There were at least three more in the parking lot amidst 20 or more similar luxury counterparts. The HSE Sport is a beautiful vehicle with a rich tradition of African safaris and humanitarian relief. Time proven as the vehicle of choice in the vast British Empire, it has gained a reputation of safely traversing through the most extreme conditions and circumstances. A nice choice, I say to myself. Admiration leads to envy as I calculate the $80,000+ price tag. As my thoughts assess my new found "need," a cost benefits evaluation leads to doubt concerning the idea of personal ownership. Well, if I can't justify it, why can my neighbors? What actually were their motives? Were they anticipating a jungle safari in the near future, a desert rescue, or a disaster recovery? I had to conclude that they had an extra $80K lying around burning a hole in their pocket, and this was an impulse purchase driven by passion and possibly vanity. Oh, the pride and self-satisfaction purchased through peer approval. Then there is the safety of owning a truly viable all-wheel-drive supercharged vehicle for secure travel over those rugged, pothole-laden interstates. Finally, there is the comfort, the luxury, and the pleasure of fine cordovan leather caressing my "assets."

Analytical by nature I did some quick mental calculations. Eighty thousand dollars at 7% is a time value cost of $5600/year which is $108/week or $15/day. This doesn't even factor in the cost of depreciation, which is huge. We can't forget the full comprehensive insurance required to protect my investment. WOW, that's expensive transportation just for a whim or ego boost. This excess triggered a memory concerning a humanitarian project I became introduced to recently.

In Ethiopia the average labor rate is $1/day. Ethiopia is a relatively safe developing country. A lot of good is happening there regarding human rights and education, but as with all developing nations, so much need is present in every facet of the life experience. In Ethiopia as it turns out, there are over 5 million AIDS orphans. One million of these kids are AIDS-affected, while the remaining 4 million are parentless because of AIDS-related death. These children are left without a loving home life and they are severely unequal in the eyes of everyone. A mere $1 a day radically changes the future of these kids' lives if placed in the hands of a caring, honest, gentle friend. I know such a couple. Drawn to Ethiopia with the goal of adoption, 15 years later they serve tirelessly aiding one child here and another there, not taking ownership but merely there to assist them. Assisting them where they live, where they will grow, where they will lead and nurture in the manner they have been taught. I asked, "How do you avoid becoming overwhelmed? For every one you assist thousands are missed." With a quivering lip and moist eye, the director responded, "Focus on the one. Appreciate what you can do for the one, and enjoy their smiles."

To change the world, change the children. This couple chose to invest in one child at a time, one day at a time, and one dollar a time. As such, they are radically changing the lives of thousands of children. Not just one child has been helped, but generations of relationships have benefitted through personal advancement and achievement. In time, myriads of souls hold their names in reverence for this life, as well as for the eternities.

Let's see, the Range Rover depreciates at a rate of 10% a year with a salvage value of 5% in 10 years. The investment of my Ethiopian saviors is an exponentially self-generating acclaim of thousands forever.

Time is the great equalizer isn't it? Whether in Ethiopia, Ecuador or Eugene, Oregon, we all are entrusted with the same daily allotment. With that time we can choose to pursue wealth, personal pleasures, and public notoriety, or we can choose to give needed service through personal sacrifice and ego surrender. We must all answer the question, "Is my investment building the legacy I wish to leave?"

60. CURRENTS

I'll begin with a confession that I'm not a great fisherman. It's a social thing for me. Men fish, that's how it is, and I accept it. My father was a great outdoorsman. He was a master of the whole hunting/gathering genre. I'm a genetic mutation. Fortunately for me, many of these primitive skills aren't required today, or otherwise natural selection would have removed me from the gene pool long ago. But, back to my story. Tim is a heck of a fisherman. He knows how to cast, where to place, and when to pull. He can even do it on a float tube. I can get by okay on the shore, but on a tube floating down a fast moving river, that's another thing altogether.

It's spring and the flow is high, the current strong. Rocks, deadfall, rapids, and switchbacks are all part of the sport. Adding to the confusion is the rod and reel. I must keep reminding myself that the objective is to catch fish so that we can then release them. Well, I'm not good by any means, but my skills have progressed to a point of marginal success. I'm in control a lot of the time, and occasionally a fish bumps onto my hook, swims up to me and then requests that I unhook him. It's all very civil.

Over time I've learned to let the current do most of the work. As needed, I make minor adjustments with my flippers. If I just let the current do its thing I'm usually a lot better off. It's moments like this where I begin to see the joy in the activity; it is peaceful, quiet, beautiful, and serene. The fish merely provide the justification for the tranquil setting and the time expended.

As I approach an unfamiliar bend, a new rapid, a rock, or a tree, momentary fear leads to panic. If care is not administered, the flippers begin to frantically maneuver my position and the situation gets out of control very quickly. The rod, the reel, and the line compound the situation. When I can remain calm I recognize that the actual flow of the current around most things will keep me safe. The worst thing that can be done is to attempt to stop in the middle. The slippery rocks and flipper-bound feet combine with the resistance of the tube against the water creating all the components needed for disaster. Oh, did I mention the rod and reel? Unconsciously, as I strive for a sense of immediate control, the feet go down and the rest is history. When I'm relaxed, a little aggressive flipper action can always get me out of impending danger or to shore and safely out of the current. Then, and only then, do I stand safely on the shore. I know all this, but in times of panic, lessons learned are all forgotten.

The current moves regardless of whether you're in it or not. My buddies are now past the bend and heading down the river. Better get back in or I'll be left behind. The transition from standing to floating is always a rush, as the buoyancy of the tube sweeps me off my feet. The feeling of stability, safety, and security is left on the shore being replaced by the uncertain feeling of floating. This is a wonderful, exhilarating feeling of helplessness as tube and current take charge. The safety of the shore comes in exchange for progression, achievement, and advancement. The spirit of the current is my destiny. It defies my logic. It often moves faster than my comfort level, around corners unseen, and near obstacles in my path. I can elect to retire to the shore at any time. I can stay there as long as I desire. While I'm on shore I'm not progressing but I won't fall either. The safety of the shore is weighed against the opportunities the river holds. There's a strange sense of purpose and destiny in the middle of the current. Eventually all of us must ride the entire course. It's up to me to determine when and how I do it.

* * * * *

61. MY ROOM

"Everyone needs a little room where they can close the door and be alone."

Paramahansa Yogananda (1893-1952)

I embark on this reflection with the qualification that applicability begins with an individual question: "How can I thrive in the rapidly changing world of today, and survive in the uncertain world of tomorrow?"

Living large and dreaming big is requiring ever more energy, and consuming all available attention. The tabloids and television media easily sway our level of contentment as our individual focus and vision skews to the pressures of our dynamic world. Looking progressive while staying straight is ever more challenging while caught in the current of this ever-demanding "beautiful life." Identifying acts of true compassion, when all compete for social attention parading around in "designer fashion," is definitely confounding the indifferent. Brutally honest introspection is the price tag when it is concluded that things aren't right, and that change is vital. The trigger to change is personal and private; the requirement for change is obvious.

To see clearly and with exactness the point where I stand in relation to where I came from and where I am headed, does not come without pain. Am I adapting to the changes being thrust upon me? Am I barely holding on? Or, am I in reality losing ground at a slow but steady rate? No longer can I be anything but perfectly honest with myself. The question must rise from within, for no other can force it. The desire for introspection is paramount because no person advances without going through the perpetual, personal X-ray. Where I am, where I desire to be, and where the earthly influences are taking me set the stage.

Development is voluntary. A positive decision to make the precise step starts with introspection. Honest assessment of strengths and weaknesses, in context of time and not factored by justification and rationalization, is the launch. Being content with a quick superficial comparison against the guy across the street will not cut it.

I've heard it said that the true laboratory is the mind for it is only here that we can actually be alone. It is here, that without intrusion, we can experience honest introspection. Self scrutiny, with the relentless observance of one's thoughts, is a stark and shattering experience. True self analysis is pulverizing to even the strongest egos, but with effort it can produce insight, perspective, and resolution.

Sitting in silence in the room of our mind forces apart the intellect from the senses, and allows us to experience things at a deeper level. The contemplative mind, attempting its return to divinity, is constantly dragged back toward the senses by the noise of the present. Controlling the mind is the avenue to the infinite. Once I am resolved to no longer allow myself to be dominated by the routine sphere of rowdy sensations and restless thoughts, I am freed from my ego-prison and can smell the fresh air of self-determination. These farsighted thoughts disengage me from physical and mental identifications in favor of personal individuality. Driven by a shallow ego, we today assume that it is us who thinks, wills, feels, digests, and sustains. We cannot acknowledge, through reflection, that in our ordinary life we are but a slave of past actions, nature, cultural norms, and expectations. Each rational reaction, feeling, mood, and habit merely reflects past circumstances. In the solitude of my mind, however, lasting truths and personal freedoms reveal my noble soul. This sensitivity destroys the ignorance imposed upon me by society. It provides a depth of personal knowledge that cannot spring up by any other means than self-inquiry.

The Indian experience of self-control explains that we must exchange unprofitable speculations for actual Higher Order communications. We must clear our minds of dogmatic theological debris; let in the fresh healing waters of direct perception. Attune ourselves to the active inner guidance, for this grander voice has the answer to every dilemma of life. Our ingenuity for getting into trouble is endless, but the Higher Power is no less resourceful. Seek truth in reflection, not just books. We must go to the room of our mind and experience the power of introspection. It is here we will find our real self. It is here that we will thrive. It is here that we will survive.

62. TIGERS IN MY MIND

The mind is the master of muscles. The body is literally manufactured and sustained by the mind. This occurs through instincts expressed as habits, which in turn are manifest as desirable or undesirable actions. The habit-bound body has the power to foil the mind. This begs the question, should the master allow himself to be commanded by the servant? Should the mind be enslaved by the body's dictation? Hindu belief suggests that not only does the mind dictate personal behavior, but it also has the potential of influencing people and things, both inanimate and organic. The mind possesses power well beyond the obvious.

As I look upon a tiger it is definitely a tiger in my mind. A Hindu philosophy teaches me to see them as pussycats. I think that I can impress upon my subconscious the thought of a tiger as a pussycat, but I don't know whether I can make the tiger believe it. One would not expect victory from a baby who imagines a tiger to be a house cat, but is it possible for a strong man to turn the tables on the tiger? Powerful hands are a significant weapon but are they enough to force the mighty cat into the belief that it is a common pussycat? The royal Bengal, in its natural fierceness and habitat, is vastly different from the drugged circus animal. Many a man with powerful strength has been terrorized into complete helplessness before the onrush of the mighty tiger. In most cases the tiger successfully converts the man to a state of fear. So how important is the mind in this equation? How significant are our thoughts and attitudes in determining our outcomes? Strength comes at great cost of time and energy, but is muscle enough? Is the mind equal, if not greater?

Again Hindu wisdom enlightens: You may control a mad elephant; You may shut the mouth of the bear and tiger; You may ride the lion and play with the cobra; You may wander through the universe and instruct the stars; You may make vassals of the gods or be ever youthful; You may walk on water and trod on fire; But control of mind is better and more difficult.

There are many kinds of tigers in our lives. Most roam the jungle of human spirit where desires and passions become victor of the inner soul. Fed meagerly, a wrathful appetite is developed, which if left unchecked can consume all. I'm caught by the thought "fear makes the tiger bigger than he really is". Subdue the beasts of ignorance roaming in the jungles of the human mind before engaging in dominance of the external (Paramahansa Yogananda, 1946).

* * * * *

63. MY DOG, HOOVER

I have a thought which I would like you to understand. Will it change your life? Probably not, but I would at least like your perspective. We talk, we write, and we act. I choose to write it with words that I'm familiar with. Hopefully they are the ones you've experienced before. Based upon life's past experiences, your conclusions may or may not represent my original intent. If we were identical twins, raised, dressed, and educated the same, we would still have misunderstandings. But what of two souls from radically different cultures, language, age, gender, and experience? It is of a surety that nothing could be fully understood, and this brings me to my dog, Hoover.

Hoover was named after the vacuum cleaner because he ate everything! Even though we are both males, of similar age (he in dog years and I in man years), and have lived in the same environment, we are still radically different. Sometimes when I'm upset I will call out the vilest names while patting his head. It doesn't phase him a bit. Happily he remains as long as I keep scratching his ears. If I boot him in the butt, fear and confusion enter his eyes and all the kind, flattering words spoken in the softest, gentlest tones don't change the meaning. When anyone in the house is sick, Hoover is by his or her side licking them with that gamey, smelling tongue. He will snuggle and cuddle without a word from anyone for as long as needed. Things seem just a little better because of his timeless companionship. He can't offer possessions, money or acclaim, but his small acts of concern are priceless due to the timing, location, and volume. Hoover's intuition appears far superior to my mind and experience.

As a global society we have become so technologically sophisticated that social interconnections never before dreamed possible, are emerging and constantly evolving. By voice, text, data, and picture we communicate effortlessly and seamlessly without a thought, and yet we have also achieved the ability to blow ourselves up a thousand times over. Amidst this avalanche of innovation we have lost the ability to understand, to sense, to perceive, and to nurture. From raging battles to domestic violence, our hostilities all appear to have the core virus of miscommunication and misunderstanding. Meanings are not in words, but rather in the lives and fabric of people with individual personalities, needs, wants, and desires. Meanings are in people who have the capacity to love, to nurture, to perceive, and to encourage. Meanings are in people just like Hoover. How important are the Hoovers of our lives? How we need more Hoovers today. Hoovers who require nothing in return but who graciously treat, as a gift, the occasional scratch or snuggle whenever it comes.

* * * * *

64. TSUNAMIS

When submarine earth movement or volcanic eruptions of 6.5 or greater occur, a huge sea wave is created. Considered one of the world's most powerful and feared forces in nature, they are often over three stories tall and travel across the ocean floor at the speed of a jet. When this wave emerges at the shoreline it can destroy a coastal city in seconds. The only way to survive is to tie yourself to something solid, hold your breath, and keep your mouth shut until it passes. Don't attempt to stand up, move around, or even look up during one as the forces are too powerful to resist. It ends as fast as it came leaving death and destruction everywhere. As soon as it's over the clean up and rebuilding can commence, but only if you survived. Because tsunamis travel on the ocean floor at such great speeds, they are undetectable until they appear, allowing little advance warning.

When emotional tsunamis collide with our personal shores, in desperation, we often try to stand up against them. In fear, we desire to defend our opinions. In anger, we justify our actions. In guilt, we attempt to rationalize our words. Disputations over facts and perspectives are part of the rebuilding process that will come in time, but today, as I witness the wall of water rise above the shore, all I can do is sit down, hold on and shut up!!!!

* * * * *

65. FORCE OR POWER?

Some time between birth and the grave, life comes into perspective, and hopefully balance is achieved. Our first noise is a reaction to physical contact. From that moment on we struggle to grow and control. Born to fight, most of us get caught up in the struggle. The competition to survive and succeed is great. A balance is necessary. Man thinks he lives by virtue of the forces he can control, but the majority of us rely on force to compensate for our feelings of powerlessness. The reality is that we are influenced by powers over which we have no control. Increasing our integrity, our understanding, and our capacity for compassion will strengthen personal feelings of power.

It's really just a battle between selflessness over self-interest. A life dedicated to charity towards others and concern for their welfare possesses power through meaning. Meaning is only lost when we run out of needy people. A life dedicated to financial success loses meaning once that is attained, leading to depression, disillusionment, and emptiness. Force brings satisfaction, but only true power brings joy.

Love, compassion, and forgiveness are mistakably seen as soft, submissive steps to self-fulfillment, when in fact they are profoundly empowering. In contrast, revenge, judgment, and condemnation are consuming and repressive. Our goal is to give up weak characteristics which enslave for empowering ones that free us. Holding forgiveness in your mind you will feel strength, while holding revenge in your heart you will be weak. By giving up forceful behaviors we thus release powerful ones.

* * * * *

66. SALE SHIRTS

The other day while waiting in line to purchase an article of clothing, my mind went back to a time many years ago. I was in high school and at the home of a friend. His father, a highly educated man who was prone to offering advice through lecture, advanced his beliefs whenever motivated, regardless of whether asked for or not.

A favorite lecture which we all especially enjoyed was the "Sale Shirt" speech. This sermon seemed to come whenever he overheard us talking about purchasing anything over five dollars. To him, a shirt was a commodity used to cover your nakedness, and so one should always get the cheapest one available. To most of us, however, wearing a nice shirt was very important as it enhanced our self-esteem and was visible evidence of how cool we were. We didn't care what the cost was. We just wanted a nice shirt or a nice car. To him a car was merely a tool to move one from point A to point B, and he always wanted to minimize his cost. To us, our limited purchases were an extension of ourselves, and it was well worth it to spend more and get the one that we wanted. It would drive him crazy to just listen to us talk, let alone if by chance we had the audacity to actually purchase something trendy, popular, or in style. To him hand-me-downs from older brothers were more than adequate, and anything above that was encouraging mere vanity. He never gave recognition for the satisfaction of feeling good, feeling progressive, and in fashion, which possibly he had never experienced.

This lecture could be adapted to literally all occasions, situations, or events from purchases to entertainment. At the time, we made great sport of re-enacting these lectures when on our own. Not through direct disrespect, but we were boys and that is what boys at that age do.

Things have changed a lot since those days. Today I find myself much more in alignment with his thoughts. I guess age and experience do that to a person. Today my needs are decreasing, not expanding. Today my excitement for the latest and greatest is offset by the stress of keeping up and staying current. Today anything that reduces apprehension and anxiety is a good thing. So yes, Elliot, your point did not fall on deaf ears. Yes, Elliot, we did listen. Too bad it took 40 years to settle in. Better late than never.

67. FIRESTORM

It's summer, five years into a drought and the wildfire season has begun. Regardless of age, race, position, or gender most have a common concern and are conscientiously trying to prevent fires on the tinderbox landscape. We've seen it before, when for no apparent reason a spark at the wrong time, in the wrong location sets the world in motion. It only takes one. If caught within the first few moments, it is extinguished without incident resulting in only minor inconvenience. But if left unattended with the right quantities of oxygen and fuel, the small spark can, in a flash, threaten the lives of all in its path. Only an idiot would add additional fuel and wind to the small flames. But that's what we figuratively do to some degree when firestorms threaten our relationships. How many blazes can be extinguished before one becomes a full-fledged firestorm, a self-sustaining hell, consuming all in its path? Such blazes generate their own wind, creating a white-hot inferno beyond anyone's comprehension. It can become a nightmare roaring through the neighborhood.

Surprisingly, such storms die as fast as they began once the fuel is consumed. But, everyone and everything caught up in the flames is a victim! A firestorm shows no mercy, ripping through relationships and damaging trust. One million memories are rapidly consumed, burnt, or scorched in the heat of the back drafts. Eventually the tears will extinguish the remaining embers. In time the landscape is cleared, possessions are removed, and properties are sold. In time we will build again. In time we will start over, but no one will ever forget the day of the firestorm for as long as we live. The terrors of the flames are burnt into our eternal souls. Hopefully we will remember the lessons of our past and be more careful during another fire season.

* * * * *

68. CIVIL UNREST

A long time ago I spent some time on the Emerald Isle. I witnessed a lot of death and destruction for such a tiny place. In middle school I remember learning that the civil unrest in Ireland was caused by religion. It was a great explanation, for it was simple and clean: the Irish were killing each other in the name of God. In high school I learned that the motive for their troubles changed from religion to socio-economic factors: the North had money and the South wanted some of it. In college, they explained that the social disturbances were due to extreme cultural regionalism. I guess after 400 years everyone had forgotten what actually started the feud. Historians have a tendency to bias their work depending upon whose side they agree with.

After living in Ireland for some time I concluded that they just hate each other. They have been fighting for so long that they have totally lost track of the original insult. To quote the Irish axiom, "Don't confuse me with the facts; my mind is made up!" Probably it is a case of someone calling someone something, and because they lived in different cities it was taken personally. After a lot of beer someone likely hit someone, which isn't that amazing when you consider the quantity of beer involved. Both sides quickly wrote ballads about the fight. Each side then reflected about it every night as they drink more beer. Once explosives were invented they got more efficient, and in retaliation could blow up each other's real estate and possessions. That's just how it is. It doesn't have to make sense because it's their land and they feel they can do anything they want with it. After four centuries there has been ample insults inflicted to both sides in justification of their specific behaviors. The sadness to the whole mess is that the original insult was insignificant compared to the loss and bloodshed that has followed. All this in defense of honor and pride.

Sad isn't it that we are so insecure that we can't just "get over it!" For some reason, maybe it's timing, gallons of testosterone or raging hormones, but certain small infractions become holy wars. Regrettably, such unrest is usually just a result of extenuating circumstances.

* * * * *

69. AVENGING ANGEL

We're known for our actions that are observable, documentable, and justifiable. From these events others seek to understand, to interpret, and to explain. These explanations may or may not actually represent reality. At best, they are a crude attempt to provide closure to those observing. Questioning also falls short of true meaning. Likewise, words are a crude attempt at providing reason, motivation, and understanding. All of us are driven by numerous factors, a few known but many not. Lying deep within the psyche are powerful forces influencing all thoughts, words, and actions. Many factors have been involved in the formation of these elements of our personality, our ego, or our subconscious self from which esteem originates. All are mere attempts at describing the inner workings of the individual mind. This "black box" is, at best, unexplainable.

Recent technical advancements have shed new light on brain research measuring activity and action. Self-producing electrical impulses and chemical secretions appear to be at the source. But, what is the link between circumstance, environment, and perceived threat that trigger these electrical and chemical excretions that in turn create muscular response? These responses then generate additional changes to the environment, initiating even more electro/chemical secretions and the cycle continues.

I was watching a documentary the other night on the History Channel that brought all this to the surface. A 52-year-old man bent on vengeance turned a bull dozer into a killing machine. Offended by the city council, his anger evolved to rage that in turn distanced the two opinions, polarizing them to the extreme. No one will ever know his true motives. Ample documents, meeting minutes, and news articles leading to the fateful day fall short of explaining his rational. One day it all came to a head when after months of solitary work he released his "killing machine" onto the streets of the little Colorado town.

The Caterpillar DT11 track type dozer was used as the basis for his invention. Weighing in at 230,000 pounds, its 850-horse engine carried the 30 foot long, 15 foot tall machine along. Equipped with a single shank ripper in the rear and a 20-foot wide front blade it was an impressive machine to begin with. For his protection he added two layers of ¾ inch steel over the cab and engine. Between the steel layers was a two inch gap which he filled with concrete, making it an indestructible bullet-proof vehicle. Three remote cameras with Lexan protective lenses provided visibility from inside the cab. Two openings at each end allowed the 10mm cannon and machine gun to be fired.

After 18 months of work this machine emerged onto the streets. Once moving, nothing was safe. Everything in its way was mangled and destroyed. Cars, trees, and street signs were devoured without hesitation. His hit list was obvious. He first targeted the city offices where a tour group of elementary children had recently left. Every member of the city counsel was under attack. From businesses to personal property, none were exempt. All went down effortlessly as if they were made of match sticks and glue. Public and private landmarks collapsed to rubble in an instant. Soon anything and everything in his way was destroyed. Completely impervious to external resistance, the local police were helpless and vulnerable. Within a few hours millions of dollars in property was destroyed, and no lives were left untouched. The local newspaper was reduced to a pile of bricks. The hardware store was next on the list. Not content to just bash in the front as in many of the other establishments, his vengeance seemed to surface here. Blow after blow was delivered. Soon it was obvious that his objective was to level the entire 100x400 foot structure. It was here that the “killing machine” met its match. Just as the local National Guard was being called in for an anti-tank missile strike, the machine came to a stand still. As it turned out one of the 14 foot tracks fell into the basement. The 24 inch clearance was not enough to prevent the machine from becoming high centered on the exposed foundation. Nothing could be done from inside the machine. Neutralized by his own obsession, he now lay helpless and motionless. As local authorities recognized the situation, they began to move in closer. Upon arrival, a muffled shot was heard from within the machine. The entrance door on top of the cab was accessible from inside the cab only. Ninety minutes were required for rescue workers to gain entrance into the cab. By then the lifeless body of the 52 year old Avenging Angel was all that remained.

So what was the point? No one will be the same. Enormous amounts of time, resources, and emotion were consumed. Vast sums of money will be required to bring things back to normal. Was anything actually gained? Was any significant issue brought to public light? Sadly, we will never know the true motivations of the Avenging Angel. All we are left with are artifacts and token elements from which to draw biased generalizations of motive and objective.

In a less racial sense aren't we all in this same predicament? No one will ever really understand our true motivations. Our obituary will be written from the observations of others. Our achievements, accomplishments, awards, and activities will be noted, but no one will truly understand the exact reasoning of our existence.

* * * * *

70. OPTIMISM

Is your glass half empty or half full? Optimism appears to be directly related to gratitude. Pessimism is aligned to thanklessness. The way I see the world, the lens through which I look will determine my level of optimism. I can get upset because idealistic plans, hopes, and desires are unfulfilled, or I can choose to see the positive aspects of these perceived failings. When things fall below my expectations I can lament, or I can regroup and try again. The degree of deficiency is directly related to the dissatisfaction experienced.

Based on academic grading standards, we live in a "C" world; not a D, thank heavens, but definitely not an A either. Despite the way that the media characterizes life, it is never quite that perfect or ideal. Illusions distort our perspectives hourly. In winning the lottery my life will not necessarily change for the better. By accepting unrealistic standards I will find myself emotionally short, making it hard to feel grateful. If I can live with difficult circumstances I should be able to live with the best circumstances.

The human spirit is adaptive by nature. Having spent time abroad, I still vividly recall the lack of common utilities and conveniences. Within a week, however, I had adapted to the strange environment. Over time an extraordinary freedom emerged due to my sense of increased resourcefulness. As a result my optimism improved.

It doesn't take a genius to be frustrated when things don't go as planned. It is easy to get irritated when life falls short of what was promised or expected. It is natural to feel sorry for ourselves when others appear to have struggled less and received more. I believe, however, that this life is a grand game of self-discovery. The true measure of success is not limited by temporal measures. We will never be happy until we cease measuring our life's achievements against others' dreams. Regardless of the outcome, I will be where I should be, where I belong, where I'm comfortable, and where I'm at peace. This is my reward for doing my personal best given my unique course. I'm now thankful just for the opportunity to play, and my optimism lies in the belief that my life is a one-of-a-kind experience tailored exactly for optimum growth and refinement.

71. WHY ME?

I came across some world statistics the other day. Accuracy may be questionable as such statistics change rapidly, but the message is crystal clear. The perspective I gained from these statistics added focus to my current challenges, and in turn I felt a sense of sincere gratitude for my condition.

If the entire world population was represented by just 100 souls, what are the chances that I would be where I am, with what I have, living the life that I have? Of the 100 individuals, four would live in the United States, eight would be African, 21 European, and 57 Asian. Fifty-two would be female and the remaining 48 male. Thirty would be white and as many would believe in God. The Americans would posses 59% of all the worlds' wealth. Twenty would live in decent housing, 30 would be literate, and half of us would be malnourished. One would be near death and one would be in delivery. Only one would have a college education and that person would own the only computer.

As I scan this data I conclude that my state isn't too bad. I am awestruck that I am where I am. Why me? What happened that I arrived in this condition? What did I do to be the beneficiary of so much of what this world has to offer? I have challenges, yes, but not like that of my fellow villagers.

In our quest for success and achievement, do we lose perspective and balance? It seems that most of the determinants of our present circumstance are actually beyond our control. The majority of our pride should be attributed to birthright rather than to personal accomplishment. Able parents and caregivers provided us with the opportunities, challenges, and gifts necessary to develop and improve ourselves. I don't know the threat of malnutrition. I live in comfortable surroundings. My car, my clothing, and my electronics are neither the best nor the worst, but at least I have them. My education has broadened my horizon and enlightened my soul. I'm healthy, strong, and free. I live in a country where I can literally go anywhere I wish, be anything I choose, and believe anyway that I want.

When I question, "why me?" it is not in discouragement or sorrow, but rather in awe and wonder that I have been so blessed.

72. I'M GRATEFUL

As I kneel in meditation this morning my heart is full. I reflect upon the last few days with gratitude. Relationships I thought once lost are returning. Not better, not worse, but unique, strong, and genuine. In my reflections I can't help but recognize how resilient the heart is. Extreme situations are handled without missing a beat. More importantly I focus upon the little effort put forth, considering the outcome. I responded to an impulse, and because the time was right and the conditions primed, positive results occurred. This is proof that our ego's hold on us is strong, but also short term. Like the fevers breaking after an extended illness, once it submits it can never command complete control again. Healthy pride is good if it is tied to personal respect and dignity. It allows us to function in today's complex and demanding society. Taken to the extreme it becomes the source of most heartache by preventing reconstruction, blocking negotiations, and killing restitutions.

Mutual desires for closeness brought us back together and initiated the mending of our fractured relationship. Simultaneous yet independent, our hearts were softened. Only then could they begin healing. I leave with new confidence, dignity, and joy. Time may pass but our renewed relationship will continue to grow. Distance may separate us, but fondness will increase. Where once paranoia, speculation, and hearsay dominated, now, reality begins to prevail. I feel a simple reassurance that misunderstandings of the past have been forgotten in the wake of desired love.

Gratitude! Yes, gratitude is felt, for I am aware of how little direct involvement I had in the process. I am merely an actor in a grand play where we personalize the parts, but inspiration dominates when allowed. The rebirth of this relationship was triggered only by a mutual willingness to come together. Uncertain of the outcome, personal fear had to be subdued. Now strong once more, we will never allow things to deteriorate again.

* * * * *

73. SUPPLICATION

There is a lot of talk out there concerning the effects of positive or negative thought, and how it affects attitudes, health, and behavior. The premise of such thought is that you are what you think. Some even claim that we each posses our own unique aura which is a field, so to speak, that radiates around our body. It is identifiable by color and is determined by mood, attitude, and expression. Similarly, the Indian Mantra and the Catholic Rosary are both repetitious chants of positive affirmations to modify thought and subsequent behavior. Can our thoughts affect our countenance? Can our emotions be detectable without word? Can attitudes determine our health?

If I allow my mind to become consumed by any aspect of current condition or past circumstance, future thought is altered. Constructive thoughts lead to positive actions, as do negative thoughts lead to harmful behavior. A healthy assessment of self is required, but if taken to the extreme it can become detrimental. To this scenario now enters the ego, that self-centered defender of pride, envy, vanity, and esteem. All or nothing in approach, either I'm great or valueless, the ego seeks to thwart my will. Left unattended it will go to the extreme, giving justification through partial and selective data.

So what about personal meditation, prayer, and perceptual conversations with an unknown source of beauty, goodness, and truth? Can this counter the negative influences of the ego? There is a great benefit to mental health that is derived from regular meditation. Does kneeling in a quiet, private setting humble the ego? Can calmly assessing life's events by searching for individual meaning improve personal perspectives? Does mental review of pending problems result in more options and sounder outcomes? Does regular examination of current challenges and opportunities improve performance? Yes, definitely yes!

* * * * *

74. ANGER MANAGEMENT

Recently I was driving south out of LA on the 405. Unfamiliar with the peculiarities of the road concerning merging and exits, I inadvertently found myself exiting. I realized the dilemma just in time to change out of the exit and back into the south bound traffic. Although my maneuver was short of ideal, it was safe and legal. A car in the lane that I merged into was nearer than I realized due to her accelerated speed. My maneuver was identified and abruptly responded to. The horn is a strange accessory. Designed as a safety devise, it has evolved from a tool for warning to one of communication. It has become a mode of expression, a vehicle of conveying sentiments well beyond the verbal. Well, I got the message and if that wasn't enough she aggressively passed on the left, then abruptly cut in front of me, then tapped her breaks. WOW! Without her help I never would have realized that I had messed up. Now I was emotionally engaged and passed on her feelings with other unsuspecting motorists on the road that day.

So, why such anger? Did I intentionally cut her off? Was my screw up taken as an act of war? Her retaliatory actions more that offset the risk I presented to her. I've heard that anger is a byproduct of fear. The greater the manifested anger, the greater the perceived fear. I honestly admit that I have been an excessively angry person to this point of my life. My aggression has led to expedition of my opinions and desires that has reinforced its use. Independent of the real or perceived virtues of my perspective, the fear of them not being accepted on their merits led to anger and subsequently greater aggression.

Events of my recent past have been a radical departure from my typical behavior. I confronted intense anger and hostility with silence and calmness. This is a drastic change from my anticipated reaction. Surprisingly, this passiveness was met with even greater anger. Generally my anger would arise out of the fear of being misunderstood. Fortunately this time I was able to talk through these instances and regain perspective and posture. Fear was replaced with sadness, remorse, and resolve to improve. I now see that the intense anger dealt me was in fact motivated by the other party's paralyzing fear of a situation spiraling out of control, combined with the inevitable change, and resulting isolation. Although there is little I can immediately do to mend the broken vase of this event, an understanding of the source of this anger enables the situation to be placed in proper perspective. This perspective frees me to focus upon the long-term relationships and not upon the hurt of the moment. Now, rather than anger directed at the lady on the 405, I feel remorse for having scared her. This simple change in perspective will not fix yesterday, but it will definitely improve my commute tomorrow.

The mind is the source of all behavior. It is the conduit to personal sensitivities and spirituality. By making time for healthy self-review, attitudes improve, countenances transform, and egos moderate. In humble and sincere appeals, with gratitude for all things, I make supplication to a Higher Power to give me ears to hear and eyes to see the things that will enable me to grow.

* * * * *

75. CHARITY

I believe that the needs which drive the human race are survival, safety, security, social affiliation, and self actualization. The order is critical. Until the preceding level is satisfied the latter cannot be attained. When the core needs are covered, most hearts turn to providing greater good beyond self. When things are plentiful and all is right within our worlds, we then have the luxury to place other's needs ahead of our own. It's when hard times hit that our primitive self emerges. Circumstances drive us deeper and deeper into self-preservation. During these dark, self-absorbed periods it is near impossible to refocus from self to another. But, if even a small personal act of service can be given to another during such times, burdens become lighter and easier to bear. I believe that those who are engaged in the service of others will be preserved. Charity to others, during the dark days, ensures appropriate acts of love in just the right measure, at just the right time. I help you, you help her, she helps me, and together we arrive.

* * * * *

76. THE PIANO

On a recent visit to my son and his family I found them engaged in an immense project. It was the restoration of a pre-1950's piano. Obviously a bar room reject, this piano was stripped down to its inner soul. It was challenging, at best, to envision its original glory. It was infested with weevils, much of the felt on the keys and hammers was gone, and the chipped and yellowed ivory definitely showed its age. The old mahogany was stressed, fatigued, and stained from a lifetime of abuse.

sensed the urgency in the air for this project the moment I arrived. My daughter-in-law plays very well and I concluded that this was the motivating factor in rebuilding the old piano. Sanding, stripping, cleaning, more sanding, and did I mention all the sanding? This went on for days. I've always been a project type of guy, but the quality of this venture was going beyond my level. Why so much care into an item of questionable value? I became concerned about their priorities and the long-term effect on their family life when so much effort was being given to a single task.

Over the course of the week, talk surfaced about a neighbor and her two daughters. "It would be nice if they could learn how to play." I persisted in questioning of the ultimate quality level of such an item. Not days ago it had been rescued from the resting place of a landfill. Now we were attempting to turn it into a concert hall piece. It sure seemed like a lot of wasted time and effort, but we were all engaged and "bonding."

It wasn't until we neared completion that I came to realize the true purpose of this piano. It wasn't destined for their home at all. The effort, labor, time, and quality were necessary because it was meant to be given to their neighbors so that their daughters could learn to play. With tears in my eyes, I couldn't have been prouder of such pure motives in this effort than if my son and his wife had been awarded the Nobel Prize for Humanitarian Relief. The love transferred in each stroke of the brush or movement of the hand exceeded all earthly possessions. With tender gratitude I acknowledge the pride I felt that day in discovering a sense of higher self in my posterity.

77. LOVE MADE VISIBLE

One of the greatest antidotes for gluttony is a prescription for gratitude. Without gratitude the thirst for abundance becomes unquenchable as attempts are made to purchase that which can't be bought: contentment! The simplest of pleasures can bring great happiness and serenity to all regardless of wealth. Gratitude is manifest in giving. Gratitude is love made visible.

In our thirst for abundance, delayed gratification may be the key indicator of emotional intellect. Thoreau stated that money is not required to buy any of the truly meaningful necessities of the soul. All our accumulations will one day be given away so why not give them NOW! The reward becomes ours in the present rather than that of the inheritors at a later time. You never see a BRINKS truck following a hearse. When we cease to give, we begin to die. To give service is the ultimate sacrifice for another. We tend to develop a love for the served. To me the truest measure of achievement is the degree to which we have learned to love and to give. Service is sharing; this is truly a measure of love made visible.

* * * * *

78. PERSONAL PEACE

My sadness engulfs me like a dense, dark fog. I am consumed, my breath is restrained, my energy exhausted, and my optimism neutralized. Questions race through my brain: How can this be? What did I do? How do I survive this moment?

My life experiences unfold like the thin layers of an onion; each successive removal reveals yet even deeper, darker thoughts. Is this my destiny? Is this my reality? Is this my reward for the pains and strains I have lived and endured up to this point? Lying tongues, half-truths, and selective amnesia have led to this state where frustration, discouragement, and insecurity have taken over. Never in all my remembrances could I have conceived a condition such as this. Bystanders sit idly by with passive concern. Vile behavior is tolerated, accepted, and condoned, enabling even grosser atrocities. Apathy of the masses consumes the occasional rational response. I am like a match flicker in a hurricane; my existence goes unnoticed by everyone but a Higher Power. Enabling behavior by the influential perpetuates the darkness, the wounding, and the loathing as if evil itself was in charge!

When will it all end? I, alone, must determine that! I, alone, through control of my thoughts, must ignore the negative actions and behaviors of others. I, alone, must maintain a timeless perspective. I, alone, must show consistency of perspective. I, alone, must repel the pessimistic voices echoing in my soul. I, alone, must open my heart to forgive not once, not twice, but without number.

Can I do this alone? Alone, I feel like clay in the hands of darkness. Alone, I become consumed in self-pity, anger, and discouragement. Alone, I must humble myself sufficient to solicit the companionship of a comforter. Alone, I must generate sufficient courage to express gratitude in the face of excruciating loneliness and pain. I must feel gratitude for my condition, good and bad. Gratitude for my opportunities both challenging and discouraging must be acknowledged before I can move forward. There must be gratitude for my beliefs, my values, and my virtues. Gratitude for my very breathe. Alone, I must sanctify myself in thought and deed to be worthy of assistance from others, from a Higher

Power. Alone, I must choose peace, personal peace at all costs. Then and only then will support be provided. Together with integrity and courage I can begin to heal. Together with humility and wisdom I can begin to grow. Together with gratitude I can perpetuate peace to self and others.

We must all learn to accept ourselves in our current condition. The negative which surrounds me cannot be overcome unless I choose a higher path. I, alone, will choose to perceive life with trepidation, or with hope. Alone, I may become self absorbed, but joined by the power of peace I can expand. I choose not to shrink, but to enlarge. I choose not to be consumed, but to be productive. I resolve this day to be at peace in spite of the darkness, the negative, and the complexities that surround me!

* * * * *

79. HANNAH

"I was born a shy Iowa farm girl," beings Hannah's description of her childhood. Now at 97 her life story is not only amazing but a testament to service, caring, self-sacrifice, and faith. Her home is overflowing with cards, letters and photos sent during the holiday season in validation of the lives touched by this amazing soul.

Born seventh of nine children with her mother having died when she was 15, Hannah was homeless at age 18. After losing the farm, her dad abandoned the family never to be heard from again. While attending a Christian youth camp soon after this defining moment, she received the call to become a missionary. Scrimping and saving she earned enough to attend Northwestern Bible School and four years later she found herself in Mexico converting Jews to Christianity. Sanctioned by the church, young Hannah was left to her own means of financial support in her selfless quest. When asked, "Did you ever go hungry?" she replied, "I never starved. I always had something." Her 34-year ministry in Mexico came to an end when one night a voice told her, "You're going to leave Mexico for good." Within the month she was driving to California in her 1954 Ford where she has spent the last 26 years serving the Jewish people.

A close friend of mine told me about Hannah and her personal impact upon her even after meeting 25 years earlier. As fortune would have it we recently found ourselves in California and decided to make the drive to Carpentaria for a meeting. Although impressed by word of Hannah's accomplishments I was not prepared for our first visit. After 97 years just to be breathing is a rare accomplishment achieved by so few, but considering her difficult life in such a hostile environment I was anticipating a hunched, emaciated 90-year person with weathered skin and a resting mind. Imagine my surprise as we were greeted by this stately, alert, beautiful woman. Convinced that it was Hannah's daughter or granddaughter, I had difficulty believing this was Hannah. At 97 she stood tall, vibrant, wrinkle-free, stylishly dressed and smiling from ear to ear. She moved gracefully and without effort, bending and twisting more fluidly than I, and she at twice my age. As we began to talk facts, names, and dates her recollection flowed as if they had happened yesterday.

Then there was her smile; oh, her big, generous and sincere smile. The greatest incongruity for me was her near wrinkle-free complexion. This was amazing for anyone half her days but when you consider 34 years in the harsh climate of Mexico, it just didn't add up. When asked what her beauty secret was she quietly replied, "I don't worry." Think about her life for a moment: completely alone, no money, no security, no safety, without family and friend in a strange land. How was she able to do this without trepidation? How did a shy, unemployed, penniless young girl from Iowa survive Mexico for 24 hours let alone 34 years? This is the real question, which must be answered. Attractive, bright, and talented she chose her life. No victims here, no insecure, self-absorbed soul caught up in self-pity. By choice she earned the opportunity to make this journey. Was it easy? The question is insulting at best. Arriving in a foreign land with no warm hands to greet her and no safe door to close, she made it. Now 78 years later she stands as a testament to her beliefs. Defying all the rules of survival, safety, security, shelter and companionship she survived on faith.

By this time in the visit I was totally engaged. My mind was racing with questions as I envisioned more and more of her story. Tale after tale had the same theme: a huge challenge confronts her and in time deliverance come and success is achieved. Always this success came in the form of nameless interventions at just the right time in just the right place with just the right connection, answer or influence. At this point in our dialogue a sense of fear and dread began settling over me as I began to personalize her experiences. How did she emotionally address the challenges without panic, depression and fear? Hannah sensed the question by my countenance and just smiled with a glow quite unique. After some uncomfortable moments that seemed to last a lifetime it hit me. Her companion, her supervisor, her partner, her landlord her friend was the Lord! As I understood she smiled even bigger. Here is the textbook story of faith. Without question she began quoting "Trust in the Lord…" I jumped in, "…with all thy heart, lean not to thine own understanding." Now we were both smiling with eyes a fire. "Acknowledge Him in all thy paths…" Wow! Tingles of confirmation spread through my body as a physical acknowledgment of the conditions and the promises Hannah received in her selfless service. As I stood in the presence of this most submissive servant I was in awe of her and humbled that I was given the opportunity to meet her. Then, as we completed the promise, "…and He will direct thy paths!" I understood the power of childlike faith.

Here, in Hannah, lives a living breathing example of God's love for all of us. So many of us spend our lives whining away with our petty concerns and pointless efforts. We're all scared speechless of mere existence, struggling daily to gain a sense of fulfillment and achievement when herein lay the simple answer: faith. It is so simple that even the wise are confounded. Here in front of me was a woman half my age confirming to me of a life well spent, a life without worry. Our connection was beyond words and I pray its impact will last beyond the moment.

Hannah's "key to health," her "fountain of youth," her "magic pill," her "secret to beauty," offered to all regardless of age, race, position and standing is simply, faith. It is accepted by so few yet with all the wealth of the ages it is succinct and simple. Faith. Yes, faith of the mustard seed. The smallest seed known to man is the mustard seed, yet when planted in fertile soil it grows to be a stately beauty. As we seek security in this world we fail to see the need for simple faith. We crave security and we spend our waking hours, years and lives in pursuit of it. Through bankable assets, retirement plans, stock portfolios, homes, jobs, positions, and tenure we spend our lives in search of security. All this is done in an attempt to control the future through the possession of tangible, though fleeting, assets. This provides a momentary sense of satisfaction and security based upon this world which is unmatched by the contentment and peace I had the great privilege of experiencing, for but a moment, with my good friend Hannah.

* * * * *

www.ingramcontent.com/pod-product-compliance
Ingram Content Group UK Ltd.
Pitfield, Milton Keynes, MK11 3LW, UK
UKHW041939190726
13854UKWH00004B/1680